MAN AND HIS IMAGES

MAN

AND HIS IMAGES

A Way of Seeing

Georgine Oeri

A STUDIO BOOK

The Viking Press New York

CONTENTS

A WAY OF SEEING

Among the things we take for granted is the fact that we see. It is generally taken for granted, in fact, that there is just one way of seeing, the natural one. Yet not only our ability to see, but also the quality, the mode of our seeing is conditioned by our training, and by cultural patterns.

A Congolese man looks at a photograph and sees a woman carrying a small motor car in her hair. That is the way he reads a Western picture which, to Western eyes, clearly shows the car to be in the distance behind the woman. Photography is really a specific visual language; it is unreadable to quite a few peoples on this globe. The visual language, the vocabulary of perspective, likewise is genuinely common only to the Western tradition.

The human eye is capable of adapting itself to respond to an infinite number of impacts. It is made to encompass and comprehend a wide variety of visual languages that man himself has devised. These languages seem not to be particularly "natural" but "man-made": inventions of the human wit, matters of personal experience and training.

Who is naturally equipped to read the subtleties revealed under a microscopic lens or a telescopic chart from Mt. Palomar Observatory, or an etching by Rembrandt? Whoever has learned seeing anything in anything has learned the seeing by himself. It is not any different with what has been accumulated here.

Art is not made for experts, and it is not made for laymen; art is made for men. This endeavor started out by pleasing an audience uninvolved with art. In the process it became obvious that what pleased me had the best chance to please an audience at large.

THE TREE

Trees are known and familiar to men everywhere; they are the fur of the earth: trees in whose shade to rest, trees to climb, trees in which birds dwell, trees which produce blossoms and fruit. The variety of trees is infinite, in kind as well as in appearance. They are recreated to stand for man's experience not only of what a tree might be, but of what man himself is. The examples on the following pages are immediately identifiable as trees, yet none of them looks like a "natural" tree; they are symbols, expressing the idea of growth, of the creative power which continually renews itself in every living thing. They are trees of life. Each artist fuses this idea with his own perception and inner experience. In order to do so he uses the means of form which we call "abstract" to transform appearance reality into human reality.

Buddha was blessed with enlightenment under this tree.
tiers of branches spread horizontally from the vertical
stem, signifying stages of his insight. The foliage at the
directed toward the sky—the Void, the Nirvana.
"Bo Tree." Stone. Seventeenth/eighteenth century. (N
Museum, Bangkok.)

Time, place, style, and medium set these three representations of trees apart, yet a similarity exists in the idea of growth. All three versions make the connection with "beginning" and "birth": Buddha's spiritual and physical births; the seed of life nestling in the center of the onion-shaped Coptic tree in the form of a rabbit, symbol of immortality.

Three
entral
top is

ational 9

Right: A tree which is also a flower vase, contained in a circle implying the all-encompassing universe. Birds and a rabbit dwell in its life-giving realm.
Coptic linen cloth with tapestry woven ornament, in colored wools. Fourth century A.D. (The Metropolitan Museum of Art, Gift of George F. Baker, 1890.)

Left: The mother of Buddha—he is seen springing out of her chest—stands on a lotus flower under a tree, which indicates her closeness to the force of life that will enlighten her son.
"Queen Mayadevi Giving Birth to Buddha." Bronze. Nepal. (Collection Riverside Museum, New York.)

In the Judeo-Christian tradition the contents of faith are intimately linked by the image of the tree; they mold and transform its meaning as it grows through the entire drama of man's fall and salvation. The connection established between the tree image and Christian mythology is so powerful that even the profane and pagan version of the Entlebuch Flag blends into the context.

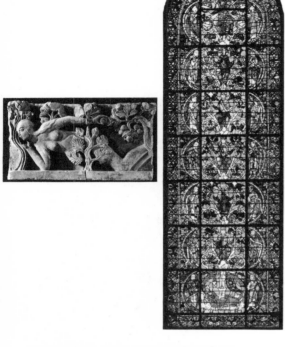

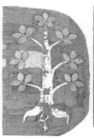

Below: The tree of Paradise behind Eve, the branches covering her nakedness, and the tree upon which she leans her head all have stems which suggest the coiling movement of a serpent. (Detail from a capital in the cathedral of Autun. Twelfth century A. D. Photo by Belzeaux-Zodiaque.)

Left and bottom left: The tree of Jesse: a genealogical tree with the connotation also of a tree of life, endlessly interconnecting the generations and culminating in the figure of the Saviour. (Details from a stained-glass window in the cathedral of Chartres. Thirteenth century.)

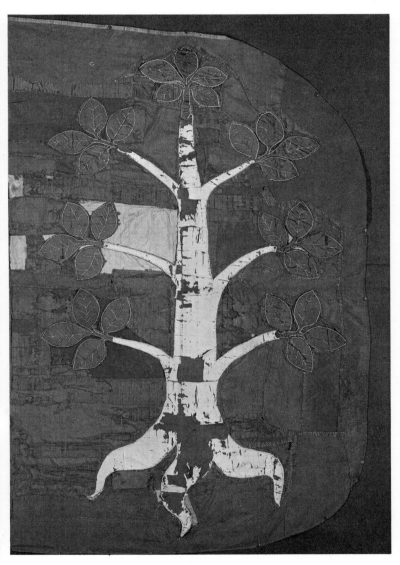

Above: A simple, terse version of a heraldic tree, assuring warriors fighting under this "flag" that they are protected by the power which gives and preserves life. (Flag of the Entlebuch County. Switzerland.)

13

The cross implies the same idea as the tree of generations of Jesse. This crucifix, although mutilated, is still a tree and still green. The water of life originates from its root in four streams.
Missal of St. Florian. Thirteenth century A.D. (Yale University Library, New Haven, Connecticut.)

The Garden of Eden is also a terrestrial, tree-filled garden. The beauty of nature is equally important as, and identical with, the Creation.
Lucas Cranach the Elder: "The Paradise." Sixteenth century A.D. (Kunsthistorisches Museum, Vienna.)

In this detail from one of five tapestries made for Anne of Brittany in celebration of her marriage to Louis XII of France, the tree stands for the bride. Keeping watch over her is a unicorn, symbol of chastity. Detail from the Unicorn Tapestries. Late fifteenth/early sixteenth century. (The Metropolitan Museum of Art, the Cloisters Collection, Gift of John D. Rockefeller, Jr.)

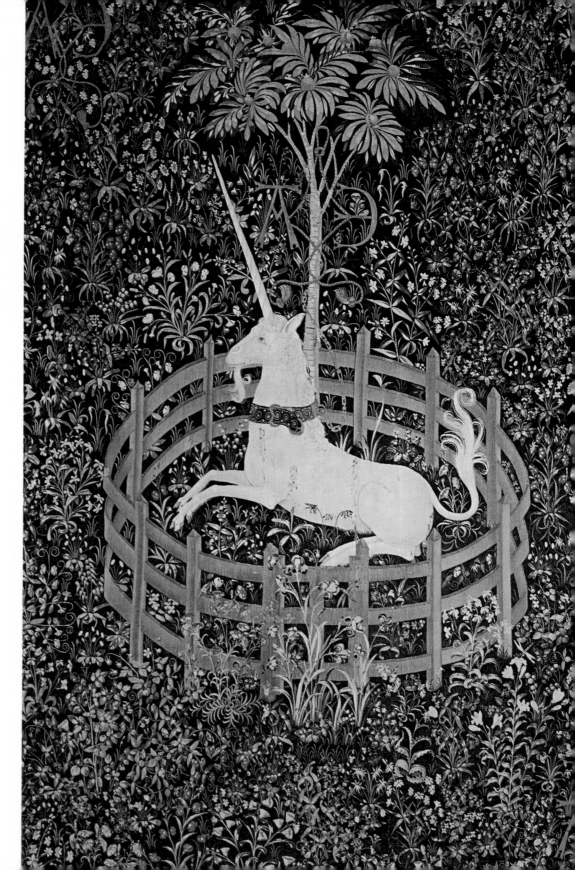

  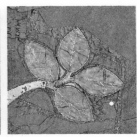   

Leaf detail
from Maya-Devi.

Leaf detail
from Eve, Autun.

Leaf detail
from Flag, Entlebuch.

Dove from
the Chartres window.

Rabbit from
the Coptic tree.

Rabbit from
Cranach's "Paradise."

While the over-all imagery of the pictures from which these details are drawn is concerned with otherworldly subjects, the small imagery reveals delight in and keen observation of terrestrial phenomena. Due attention must be paid to the dove, if it is to manifest the presence of the Holy Ghost, and to the hare, if it is to carry with it the assurance of eternal life.

A crown-shaped tree set in perfect ornamental balance. The artist, a member of the Shakers, said, "The spirit showed me plainly the branches, leaves, and fruit . . ."
"The Tree of Life." Water color. 1854. (From the original collection of Shaker Inspirational Drawings brought together by the late Edward Deming Andrews and his wife, Faith Andrews.)

Opposite: The summer heat of southern France is transformed into the blazing fervor of the artist's praise of creation. Sun and moon, the light of day and the illumination within the darkness, are present at once.
Vincent Van Gogh: "Road with Cypresses." Oil. Saint-Rémy. 1890. (Kroller-Muller State Museum, Otterlo.)

Rabbit from "Lady and Unicorn" tapestry.

TOWARD ABSTRACTION MONDRIAN — KANDINSKY — PICASSO

It is obviously valid to say that art has always been abstract. However, this realization alone is not sufficient to enable one to understand what happened around the turn of this century when what we call "modern" art was born. The entire creative generation of the time turned away from representation of the object world, and abandoned illusionist spatial organization.

The event was as drastic as the transition from the medieval representation in the flat plane (and golden ground) to the invention of perspective. And the effort to achieve it was equally difficult and painful. The

Opposite:
An example of what Mondrian finally arrived at in his maturity.
Piet Mondrian: "Composition 2." Oil. Paris, 1922. (The Solomon R. Guggenheim Museum Collection.)

Vincent van Gogh: "Road with Cypresses." Oil. Saint-Rémy. 1890. (Kroller-Muller State Museum, Otterlo.)
Claude Monet: "Poplars." Oil. 1891. (The Metropolitan Museum of Art, Bequest of Mrs. H. O. Havemeyer, 1929. The H. O. Havemeyer Collection.)
Piet Mondrian: "Tree in Landscape." Oil. C. 1905. (Collection Municipal Museum, The Hague.)

The three pictures record, in different ways, a unique moment: the phenomenal world is about to vanish in favor of the representation of realities other than visible ones. Van Gogh overwhelms the landscape with his emotional agony, so that what is really significant in the picture is the artist's experience rather than what he ostensibly shows. We are participating in Van Gogh's condition more than in a specific countryside.

Monet and Mondrian, on the other hand, clarify their direct experience of a particular subject in order to bring it into the realm of geometric laws. The particular site becomes no less incidental than it was for Van Gogh; here, however, it is utilized for the sake of evidencing an impersonal order.

paintings themselves are eloquent testimony to that fact, as shown, for example, by a comparison of Uccello's "Rout of San Romano" on page 141 with Picasso's "Demoiselles d'Avignon" on page 87.

Changes of such a basic nature are not hazarded by adventurous and innovative individuals just for the sake of creating "something new" or effecting an arbitrary change of "style". They are much too hard to bring about.

What is involved in this kind of search is a basic modification, not of one man's view, but of all men's view of the world at a given time. Mental, technical, and economic changes move men to create a new mapping of the human environment. Different interests force a change of focus, and hence a shift in the general vision of men.

The unquestioned "that's-the-way-things-look," and the confidence in it, are challenged and eventually replaced. It is not only a matter of what is or is not visible, but also of what the artist regards as important enough to be registered and recorded.

This change in vision is not to be confused with the erratic, subjective changes of personal style an individual artist may decide to make. If this were so, one would have to accuse Mr. Leon Battista Alberti of personal whim for instituting the vocabulary of perspective which, it turned out, has been adopted by every artist of the Western tradition until the end of the nineteenth century.

The transformation back to the flat plane in picture making reflects a similar general and impersonal shift in world experience. This reassessment gradually took hold of man's consciousness through the work of

Mondrian

The subject of the tree reappears—this time in the search of a single man. It is really a touching pursuit of "what is"; what is in essence rather than in appearance.

The man's name is Piet Mondrian (1872–1944), a Dutchman, for whom the utterly flat countryside of Holland and the rolling sea were the primary experiences of youth. He became

many artists working simultaneously and independently, unknown to one another until their major work was done.

The remarkable thing about this collective yet solitary effort is that it did not start out as a deliberate attempt to develop a vocabulary of abstract forms; but rather as individual artists wrestling with the representation of the empirical world. They scrutinized it, then assailed it with an intensity and insistence bordering on desperation, for the representation of purely physical appearances proved to be utterly inadequate to the reality they knew.

In an endeavor similar to that of contemporary physicists, who explored the nature of matter by attacking it and breaking it down to ever smaller units until they found that they were dealing with pure energy, the artists analyzed the world of material things and shattered it until it revealed the essentials—energies, forces, light, structures, and forms. These were the means which made it possible for them to deal pictorially with mental and psychological realities which, although less tangible, were equally authentic as human fact.

Three key figures of this period are Mondrian, Kandinsky, and Picasso. Mondrian's strict geometric poetry is a most austere renunciation of sensory reality for the reality of absolute order.

Kandinsky set free the energies of color and form, utilizing them as "objects" or components to build a composition similar to a musical composition. He recognized states of consciousness as an authentic pictorial subject, and the possibility of giving expression, by pictorial means, to states of mind.

The Mediterranean common sense of Picasso may account for the fact that he could never abandon the terrestrial delights of everyday things, for to him they are identical with the delights of spirit and mind. The phenomenal world is his oyster. Picasso probably experiences a bite of the divine when he bites an orange. He never relinquishes the immediately perceivable, yet he takes it into the realm of total symbolic relevance.

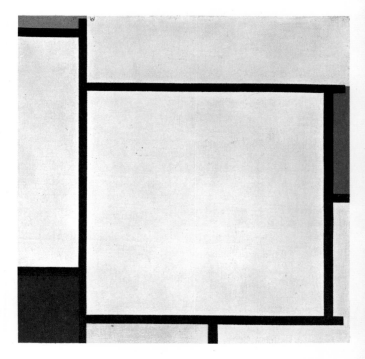

fascinated with trees; fascinated with the victory of upright growth over the overwhelming extension of the endless plains, patterned only by the equally flat surfaces of canals. As Mondrian kept working he became less and less concerned with making a semblance of a particular tree, and more and more interested in making a picture. A picture, that is, of the meaning which any tree—in fact, any experience of visual reality—revealed to him. This meaning became the subject and content of Mondrian's pictures.

He abandoned the outward likeness in favor of a symbolic image: the image of the reality of all growth, of life itself, manifested in the contrast between vertical and horizontal forces, which he called "the equivalence of opposites."

The gradual transformation of a theme, so obvious in retrospect in the following sequence of pictures, was not at all obvious to Mondrian at the time.

It is fascinating that the artist at work displays a knowledge unknown to him. Mondrian's two basic and deep experiences of nature —the tree and the sea—merge and come to.

The artist's attention is concentrated on the structure of the tree branches, the triangular shape of the tree crown. The areas of sky in between the branches are "active" forms in their own right. Color, limited to red and blue, is used to emphasize structure.
Piet Mondrian: "The Red Tree." Oil on canvas. 1910. (Collection Municipal Museum, The Hague.)

An intensified structural study, in which color is of no concern. The artist builds a dome of interrelated structural members, or forces.
Piet Mondrian: "Tree." Charcoal. 1910–11. (Collection Municipal Museum, The Hague.)

The entire picture surface now becomes a "field," a network of waves of energy. This "field" is held on the surface of the picture plane. There is no perspective depth.
Piet Mondrian: "The Grey Tree." Oil on canvas. C. 1911. (Collection S. G. Slyper Municipal Museum. The Hague.)

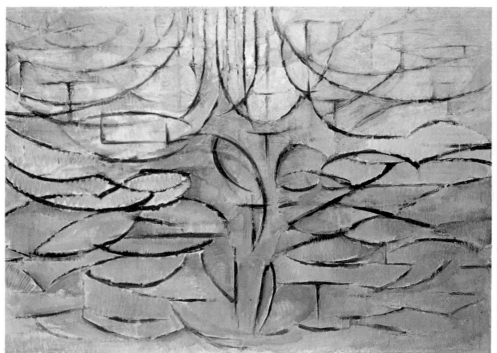

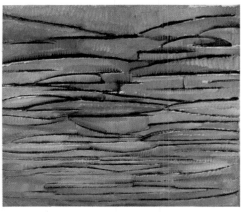

The idea of a field of forces bound to the picture plane is developed further. A definite center emerges which coincides with the center of the picture, a crossroad for all the forces running to the edges.
Piet Mondrian: "Apple Tree in Blossom." Oil on canvas. C. 1911. (Collection Municipal Museum, The Hague.)

rest in what he experienced as universal: the basic given-ness of the tension between vertical and horizontal; the basic given-ness of man's fate to be riveted to the cross of space-time. In the same way that the sea-image is embedded in Mondrian's "Apple Tree in Blossom," the tree image is interwoven in his "Pier and Ocean".

Left: A first synthesis between horizontal and vertical forces and their unending balancing inter-play, based on the shape of the cross. Honey and tan colors and various grays fill the spaces between the black line network.
Piet Mondrian: "Composition 7." Oil on canvas. 1913. (The Solomon R. Guggenheim Museum Collection.)

Left: The ripples of the sea as they decrease, for the human eye, into the distance are used for this study of horizontal movements. They are built up not into illusionary depth, but as a vertically rising structure on the picture sur-face.
Piet Mondrian: "The Sea." 1912. Oil. (Private Collection Buenos Aires.)

Above: The tree form reappears, but derived from another visual experience: the pattern formed by currents of water around a pier jutting into the sea. Observa-tions made in different areas of nature fuse in the reality they share: the universal law of "the equivalence of opposites".
Piet Mondrian: "Pier and Ocean." Charcoal. 1914. Collection S. G. Slyper. (Municipal Museum, The Hague.)

Above right: Finally, Mondrian called pictures simply "composi-tions". The reality with which this picture is concerned is a reality of the human mind. It is a "mental tree". It stands for all living organisms: they have to solve the problems of harmoniz-ing opposing forces.
Piet Mondrian: "Composition." Oil on canvas. 1916. (The Solo-mon R. Guggenheim Museum Collection.)

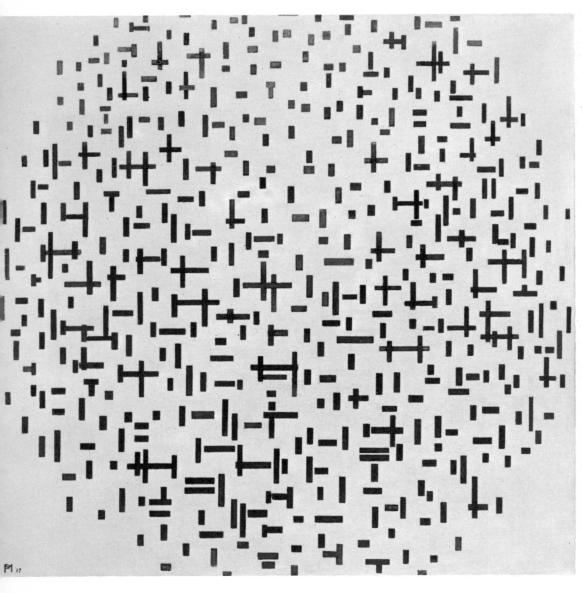

Opposite: The law of gravity is challenged —a pivoting diamond maintains balanced tension. The significance of Mondrian's contribution to symbolic image making in our time was widely recognized only after his death. He died in poverty and near anonymity in New York City in 1944. Piet Mondrian: "Composition with Blue." Oil. 1926. (Philadelphia Museum of Art: A. E. Gallatin Collection.)

"Fields" (in primary colors plus white) and "forces" (in black) combine in a state of balanced tension. Piet Mondrian: "Composition 2." Oil. 1922. (The Solomon R. Guggenheim Museum Collection.)

"Plus-minus" evokes the relationship of positive and negative elements of electricity—representing complementary opposites. The pluses and minuses activating this "field" divide and unify the composition at the same time. Piet Mondrian: "Composition with Lines (Plus-Minus)." Oil. 1917. (Collection Rijksmuseum Kroeller-Mueller, Otterlo.)

Paul Klee (1879–1940) was of the same generation as Mondrian. He was born in Berne, the son of a German musician, and became an expert violinist as well as a painter. Klee once said that his aim was not only to capture the order of rest but, beyond that, the order of movement. By this he meant that the only thing which is constant is change. In his own way Klee was looking for the same thing that Mondrian was searching for—a valid order in the world of appearances. But while for Mondrian this turned out to be permanence, for Klee it was change. As one of the keenest observers of things in the process of transformation, Klee was infinitely inventive in expressing growth and development, as is displayed in the two examples shown below. They are variations on the theme of continual growth, and express the simultaneous presence of seed and fruit, birth and death, beginning and end, in the fabric of life.

Paul Klee: "Park Near Lucerne." Oil and tempera. 1938. (Collection Klee Foundation, Berne.)

Paul Klee: "Deep in the Forest." Oil and tempera. 1939. (Collection of the State of Nordrhein Westfalen, Düsseldorf.)

23

Everyone has seen trees; nobody has ever really seen the tree of life. Yet peoples of different times and places have agreed that it exists. The two previous chapters have shown how artists have given it visible existence: they used their experience of natural trees to create a mental, a psychological, image of a reality for the human mind. In this way, the artist makes the invisible reality visible.

With the discoveries of Freud the reality of the human mind has become more tangible: we conceive of it in

Kandinsky

Wassily Kandinsky: "Amsterdam." Oil. 1903.

(The Solomon R. Guggenheim Museum Collection.)

Claude Monet: "Two Haystacks." Oil. 1891. (Courtesy The Art Institute of Chicago.)

Dmitri Kardovsky: "Portrait of Marya Anastievna Chroustchova." Oil. 1900. (The Solomon R. Guggenheim Museum Collection.)

patterns, images. With the discoveries of modern physics material reality has become less tangible: we conceive of it as invisible structures. Both of these developments have had their effect on the reality art visualizes.

With the generation of artists like Mondrian, we have ventured into making images of the realities of the human mind as direct creators. The artist creates them without using the pattern of already created things. Although science has contributed much to the understanding of psychological language, with each individual, inner vision is different, and the projections artists make on canvas frequently offer a challenge to the viewer's intellect. Wassily Kandinsky (1866–1944), a contemporary of Mondrian, exemplifies the struggle of an artist engaged in intellectual discovery and interpretation.

When the successful Doctor of Law Kandinsky, turning thirty, stood before a picture by Claude Monet, he could not figure out what it was he was looking at. This was in Moscow in 1895. "That it was supposed to be a haystack," Kandinsky wrote years later, "I learned from the catalogue. I was unable to recognize it. I was annoyed and embarrassed... I felt that the painter had no right to be so inarticulate and obscure. Yet," he continued, "this picture impressed itself indelibly upon my memory and it reappeared, time and again, to the last detail before my inner eyes." What had struck Kandinsky, although not yet consciously, was that a picture of an object could make a stronger impression on the mind than the object itself.

A year after his encounter with Monet, Kandinsky turned down a professorship of economic law and went to Munich to study painting. He learned the trade in the manner of the old masters. While the above portrait of a Russian lady of his acquaintance (until recently the painting was actually attributed to him) is not of his hand, it documents in spirit and style how and what he learned. Kandinsky was dissatisfied with this classic approach to painting and started to search for something new.

Wassily Kandinsky: "Bavarian Mountains with Village." 1909. Oil. (Collection of R. S. Zeisler.)

Wassily Kandinsky: "Autumn." Oil. 1911. (Collection of Mrs. Lora F. Marx, Chicago.)

Wassily Kandinsky: "Improvisation 28." Oil. 1912. (The Solomon R. Guggenheim Museum Collection.)

After his studies in Munich, Kandinsky traveled widely; he kept on painting, and many years later he settled down once more near Munich. In his memoirs, published in 1913, Kandinsky speaks about "wandering around with my painting utensils with the instinct of a

Wassily Kandinsky: "Study for Composition II." Oil. 1910. (The Solomon R. Guggenheim Museum Collection.)

hunter… I barely thought of houses or trees, I set bands and dabs of color onto the canvas… and induced them to sing as powerfully as I knew how.… Later, once at home, my colors were invariably a profound disappointment to me; they seemed weak and dull… an unsuccessful attempt to capture the essence of nature. How strange did it sound to me to be told that I exaggerated the colors of nature and that this very exaggeration made my pictures unintelligible." At the same time, a time of "frustration and disappointment," Kandinsky was engaged in studio work from memory and recollection. "I already searched, more or less consciously, for compositional structure. The mere word 'Composition' moved me and, later in life, it was to become my aim to paint a 'Composition'."

This picture is placed on its side—the way Kandinsky saw it one day in his studio, leading to his interest in the whole question of composition. See text on opposite page. Wassily Kandinsky: "Landscape Near Murnau." Oil. 1909. (The Solomon R. Guggenheim Museum Collection.)

Right: Wassily Kandinsky: "Black Lines." Oil. 1913. (The Solomon R. Guggenheim Museum Collection.)

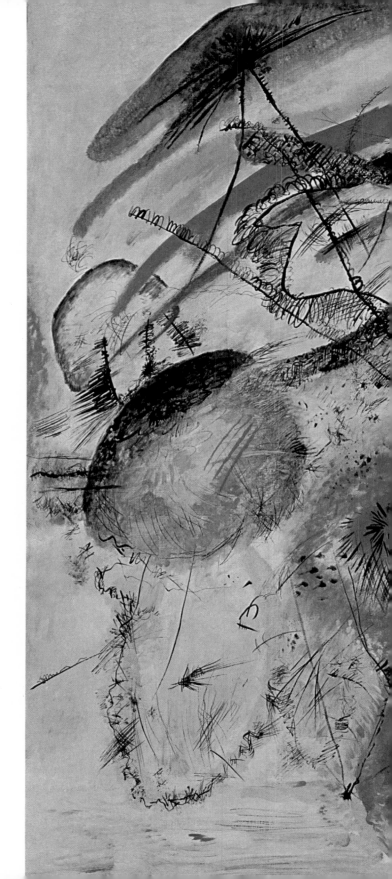

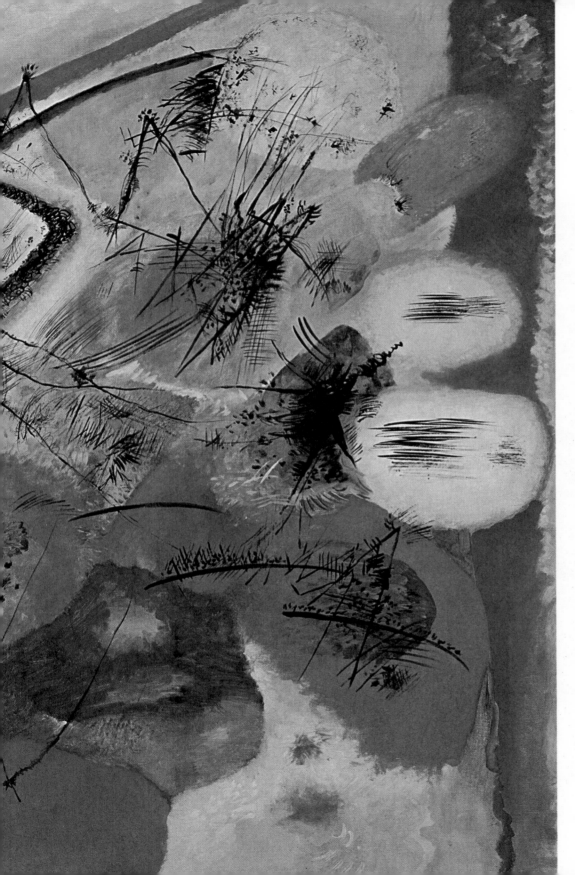

To compose meant to capture something beyond the visible world, where objects such as houses and trees would no longer stand in the way of the essence of nature. "I once found myself surprised by an unexpected sight in my own studio," he wrote. "I suddenly saw an indescribably beautiful painting, permeated by an inner glow. Taken aback, I approached the mysterious picture in which I could not recognize anything but forms and colors. It hit me at once: I was looking at one of my own landscape paintings leaning on its side against the wall."

At that moment, Kandinsky discovered that while he had been laboring on his recalcitrant landscapes, he was, in fact, already making compositions. "Now I knew with certainty that the object harms my paintings... The insight was terrifying. A multitude of questions rose before me. The most important: what is to take the place of the object? ... Many years had to pass until, through intuition and contemplation, I arrived at the simple insight that the ends (and hence also the means) of nature and art differ essentially, organically and by virtue of a universal law."

"A line is just as much as a table."

"Painting is a violent clash between different worlds which, in and through the struggle with each other, are destined to create the new world. Technically speaking, each work of art comes into being as the cosmos did —out of catastrophe. Out of a chaotic blaring of the instruments a symphony finally emerges, called the music of the spheres. The creation of a work is the creation of a world."

Left: Wassily Kandinsky: "Dominant Curve." Oil. 1936. (The Solomon R. Guggenheim Museum Collection.)

Right: Wassily Kandinsky: "Painting with White Forms." No. 146. Oil. 1913. (The Solomon R. Guggenheim Museum Collection.)

Wassily Kandinsky: "Several Circles." Oil. 1926. (The Solomon R. Guggenheim Museum Collection.)

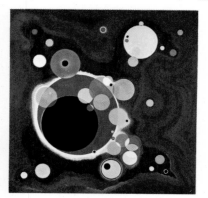

Wassily Kandinsky: "Two Sides Red." No. 427. Oil. 1928. (The Solomon R. Guggenheim Museum Collection.)

Picasso

To arrange pictures in sequence can be dangerous, because the viewer's vision is arbitrarily channeled. A picture is a world; to associate it with other pictures can diminish its singularity.

No picture is made with the intention of comparison or competition with another picture, but the risk is taken here because the sheer accumulation of formal wealth makes explicit this artist's capacity to generate form upon form. There is a basic kinship among all of Picasso's shapes; they constitute his handwriting, they reveal the "Gestalt," the inadvertent similarities, the preference for certain rhythmic cadences which keep returning in a changed context and meaning.

The rendering of the object yields to the creation of form as the "message." The devouring of the object results in its dissolution and the birth of form as magic.

"Family of Saltimbanques." Oil. 1905. (National Gallery of Art, Washington, D.C., Chester Dale Collection.)

"Les Demoiselles d'Avignon." Oil. 1907. (Collection, The Museum of Modern Art, New York. Acquired through the Lillie P. Bliss Bequest.)

"Mother and Child." Oil. 1922. (Alex L. Hillmann, New York.)

"The Meal." Oil. 1953. (Collection of the artist.)

"Seated Woman." Oil. 1927. (James Thrall Soby, Farmington, Conn.)

"Dream." Oil. 1932. (Collection of Mr. and Mrs. Victor W. Ganz.)

"Girl Before a Mirror." Oil. 1932. (Collection, The Museum of Modern Art, New York. Gift of Mrs. Simon Guggenheim.)

Picasso's fame has developed on the strength of the sheer quantity of a multifarious production and in the wake of a legendary life lived with spectacular zest. However, Picasso's fame all but obscures Picasso's real significance. He rebuilds, reshapes, re-creates the world of our experience, the empirical world.

He takes hold of our ashtrays and pipes, our dishes, flowers, and fruit, our very bodies and faces, and puts them through the most excruciating contortions in order for them to re-emerge with a new, an emphasized and overbearing presence.

One of the keys to Picasso's work are Picasso's eyes. While most of us see through the screen of convention, Picasso is able to see what he sees, directly and with innocence, and he has the capacity to make his pictorial reality in the image of what he sees. Seeing, in his singular case, means to devour the world, to consume it, because he loves it, because he finds it unceasingly and limitlessly exciting, because it is so magnificent. It is a process without mercy, but with love. Picasso is like the terrible Earth Mother who devours her own children out of her devastating fecundity.

"Landscape." Water color. 1908. (Hermann and Margrit Rupf Foundation, Kunstmuseum, Berne.)

"Still-life with Gourd." Oil. 1909. (Collection of Gertrude Stein, Paris.)

"Daniel-Henry Kahnweiler." Oil. 1910. (The Art Institute of Chicago.)

"Three Musicians." Oil. 1921. (Collection, The Museum of Modern Art, New York. Mrs. Simon Guggenheim Fund.)

Compassion—without sentiment—is the subject. The artist brings all shapes to the picture surface so that, through its heightened clarity, each form achieves readability on the plane. Shadows are negligible, or they are turned into forms such as that to the right of the feet of the small boy.

Pablo Picasso: "Family of Saltimbanques." Paris, 1905. Gouache. (National Gallery of Art, Washington, D.C., Chester Dale Collection.)

32

The table leg is given the same validity as the human leg adjacent to it,
so that both become part of an intricate web of forms.
Pablo Picasso: "Three Musicians." Oil on canvas. 1921. (Collection,
The Museum of Modern Art, New York, Mrs. Simon Guggenheim
Fund.)

33

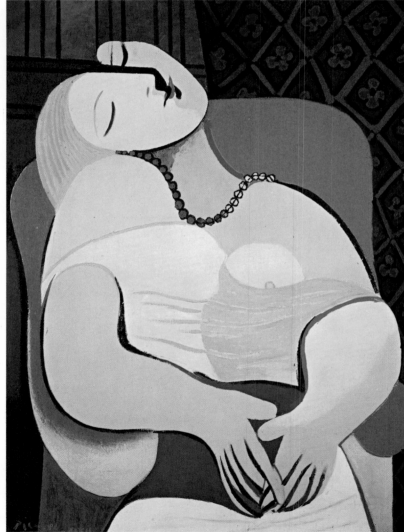

Above: What takes place in the studio of an artist like Picasso? The process of creation: the destruction of the familiar look of things—not the destruction of the things themselves.
Pablo Picasso: "The Studio." Oil. 1927–28. (Collection, The Museum of Modern Art, New York. Gift of Walter P. Chrysler, Jr.)

34

Opposite: The girl encounters more than her reflection: an awesome confrontation takes place between her day-side and her night-side, with her origin, past, and future.
Pablo Picasso: "Girl Before a Mirror." Oil. 1932. (Collection, The Museum of Modern Art, New York. Gift of Mrs. Simon Guggenheim.)

35

Guernica, a town in the Basque region of Spain, was destroyed by German planes flying for Franco during the Spanish civil war. The mural Picasso was commissioned to execute for the Paris World's Fair in 1937 became a grim memorial. Picasso: "Guernica." Oil on canvas. 1937. (Collection, The Museum of Modern Art, New York.)

These details reveal a persistence of recurrent "mannerisms" as though they were inevitable. Yet the vision is always fresh: the way he "sums up" eyes and ears!

Picasso: "The Bull." Eight lithographs. From appearance to essence.

38

THE INNER LANDSCAPE: THE ABSTRACT EXPRESSIONISTS

The work presented in the previous chapter was by artists for whom Paris was the focal point of all artistic energies.

With the following group a new location comes into focus, where a new art is born. The location is New York and the art is that of the New York School. It has also been called The New American Painting, or Action Painting, or Abstract Expressionism.

This new development began in the mid-forties with the work of a small group of men who were at that time completely unknown to a wider public. Since then Abstract Expressionism has grown into a movement which has gained international recognition and fame.

The small and incomplete selection presented on these pages introduces examples of work by artists, most of whom belong to the initial group who made a revolutionary contribution to artistic expression. As much as their styles differ, their statements which here accompany their pictures have something in common: the conviction that they have the right to their own truth, and the obligation to find their own expression for that truth.

The singular situation in which these men found themselves was that the previous artistic generation had provided a complete formal vocabulary independent of the empirical, representational world and its forms. This "ready-made," abstract body of forms led to the birth of the first genuine American painting which found an expression for the "making of Americans" synonymous with creation of the world and the creation of self. The physical discovery made by Columbus found a repetition in the artists' discovery of both the world and the self, as an identical, existential experience.

"The progression of a painter's work, as it travels in time from point to point, will be toward clarity: toward the elimination of all obstacles between the painter and the idea, and between the idea and the observer. . . . Silence is so accurate." Mark Rothko (*1904).
Mark Rothko: "Number 8." Oil. 1962. (Collection of Mr. and Mrs. Burton Tremaine, Meriden, Connecticut.)

Opposite: "I felt it necessary to evolve entirely new concepts [of form and space and painting] . . . To be stopped by a frame's edge was intolerable; a Euclidean prison had to be annihilated." Clyfford Still (*1904).
Clyfford Still: "Number 3." Oil. 1951. (Collection of Mrs. Betty Parsons, New York City.)

41

Stuart Davis: "Colonial Cubism." 1954. Oil. (Collection Walker Art Center, Minneapolis, Minn.)

Opposite: Stuart Davis: "Cliché." Oil. (The Solomon R. Guggenheim Museum Collection.)

43

"Some painters, including myself, have found that painting . . . is a way of living. . . . Those artists do not want to conform. They only want to be inspired." Willem de Kooning (*1904).

Above:
Willem de Kooning: "Gotham News." 1955. Oil. (Albright-Knox Art Gallery, Buffalo, New York, Gift of Seymour H. Knox.)

44

"It was necessary for me to utterly repudiate so-called 'good painting' in order to be free to express what was visually true for me." Adolph Gottlieb (*1903).

Adolph Gottlieb: "Exclamation." Oil. 1958. (Courtesy, Mrs. Adolph Gottlieb.)

Overleaf: "I prefer to tack the unstretched canvas to the hard wall or the floor. On the floor I am more at ease. I feel more at ease. I feel nearer, more a part of the painting, since this way I can walk around it, work from the four sides, and literally be in the painting." Jackson Pollock (1912–56).

Jackson Pollock: "One." Oil on canvas. 1950. (Collection of Mr. and Mrs. Ben Heller.)

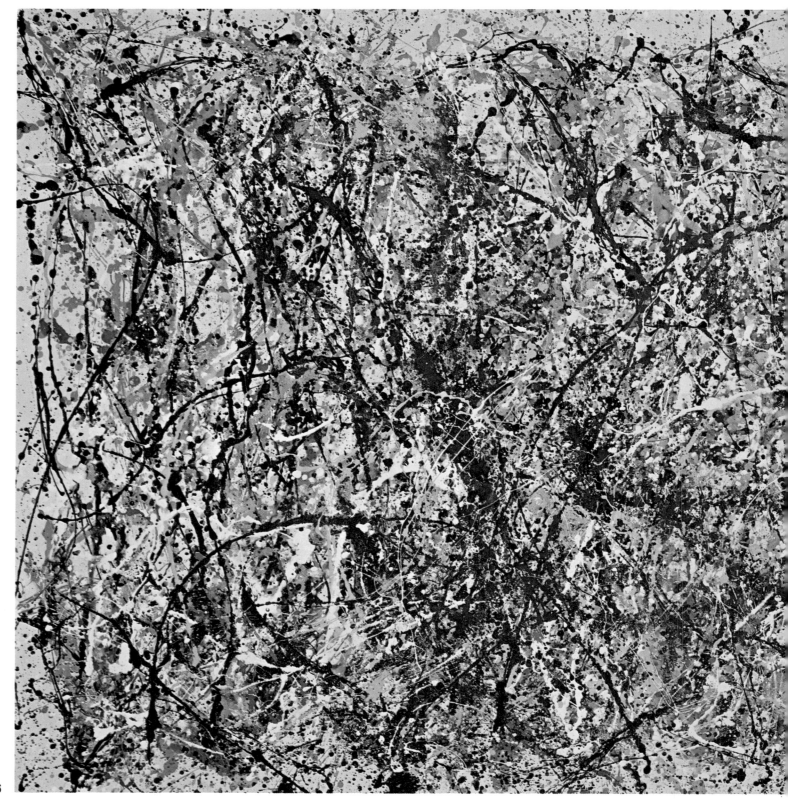

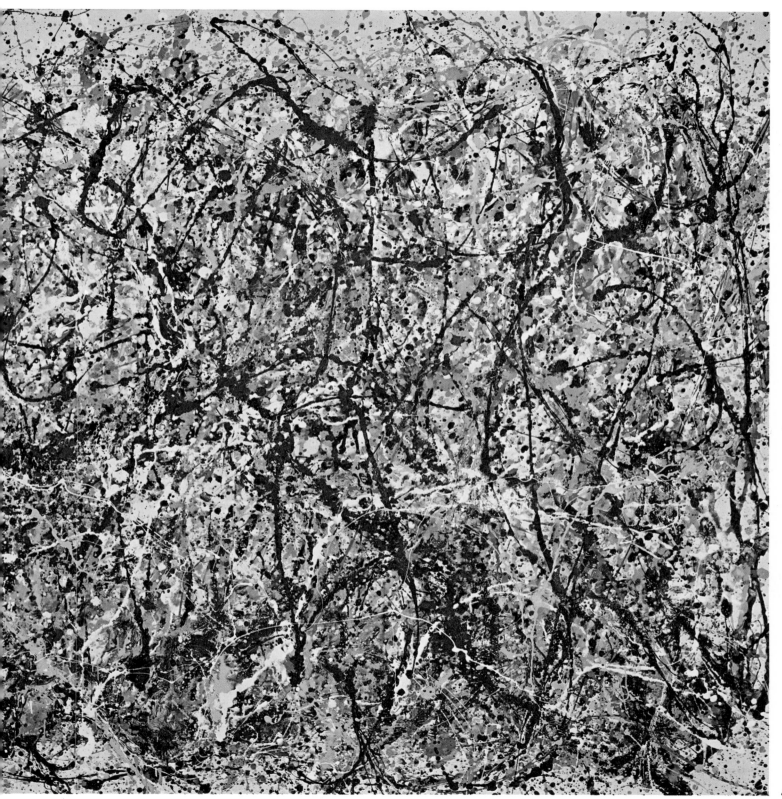

47

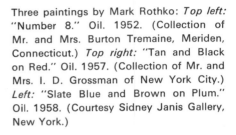

Three paintings by Mark Rothko: *Top left:* "Number 8." Oil. 1952. (Collection of Mr. and Mrs. Burton Tremaine, Meriden, Connecticut.) *Top right:* "Tan and Black on Red." Oil. 1957. (Collection of Mr. and Mrs. I. D. Grossman of New York City.) *Left:* "Slate Blue and Brown on Plum." Oil. 1958. (Courtesy Sidney Janis Gallery, New York.)

Opposite: "My hope is to confront the picture without a ready technique or a prepared attitude; to have no programme and, necessarily then, no preconceived style. To paint no Tworkovs.... The fashioned person is already limited enough—the hope is to be fashioned by the work." Jack Tworkov (*1900).

Jack Tworkov: "West 23rd." Oil. 1963. (Collection, The Museum of Modern Art, New York.)

"You don't paint the way someone, by observing your life, thinks you have to paint. You paint the way you have to in order to *give,* that's life itself.... When you have finished giving, the look surprises you as well as anybody else...." Franz Kline (1910–62).

Right: Franz Kline: "Cupola." Oil. 1958–60. (Collection Art Gallery of Ontario, Gift from the Women's Committee Fund, 1962.)

Left: Franz Kline: "Andrus." Oil. 1961. (Courtesy Sidney Janis Gallery, New York.)

Right: Franz Kline: "Painting No. 7." Oil. 1952. (The Solomon R. Guggenheim Museum Collection.)

THE HUMAN FIGURE

The practice of abstraction in art is very old and venerable. It is an integral part of the human tradition; it is, in fact, as old as mankind itself. The panorama of human figures which unfolds in the following pages begins with traces of human existence which show that whoever made and left these effigies for our contemplation was not interested in physical accuracy—the exact study and rendering of the body in terms of muscles and bones as scientific insight understands it.

The powerful, overbearing reality of the human psyche, its anguish, its search for support for its survival, embodies itself in powerful images which assert the power of renewal, of self-generation. Procreative organs are fused with and take over for the human body as a whole. These things, created by the human hand and raised to detached partnership, become objects of worship, idols to turn to for protection. The images of gods and ancestors realize the possibility of detachment.

The oval and the rod, simple and inexhaustible shapes, appear formed by man "from the beginning." They are at the origin of the violin-shape as well: Man draws the sound of harmony out of the fusion of male and female principles. (Cf. page 21: Mondrian's "equivalence of opposites.")

Through them, physical and divine at once, human survival is assured. The uninterrupted effort of man to keep that record makes for its continuity.

On the other hand, it may be open to question whether the very abundance of evidence of man's existence disguises more than reveals the nature of who and what he is! That question becomes even more open when one considers the hazards against which survived what might be boldly regarded as the imagery record of human existence.

From the monumental, although fragmentary imagery of man about man which exists, and which in itself adds an indefinite dimension to whatever idea man may have about himself, almost any notion or concept as to his real being, meaning, or character is possible.

That man keeps representing himself in ever different aspects in turn modifies his image of himself continually.

Right and overleaf: Venus of Lespugue. Found in cavern of Rideaux, S. France. Aurignacian-Perigordian era. *C.*60—40,000 B.C. (Musée de l'Homme, Paris.)

Overleaf, center: Artemis Ephesia. Marble, 168 cm. high. Discovered during excavations in Ephesus, coast of Asia Minor, in 1956. First century. (Archeological Museum, Seljuk, Turkey.)

Overleaf, right: Male (ithyphallic) statuette. Ivory. El'Amrah, Egypt. Early Nagadah period. *C.* 3400—3100 B.C. (Cairo Museum.)

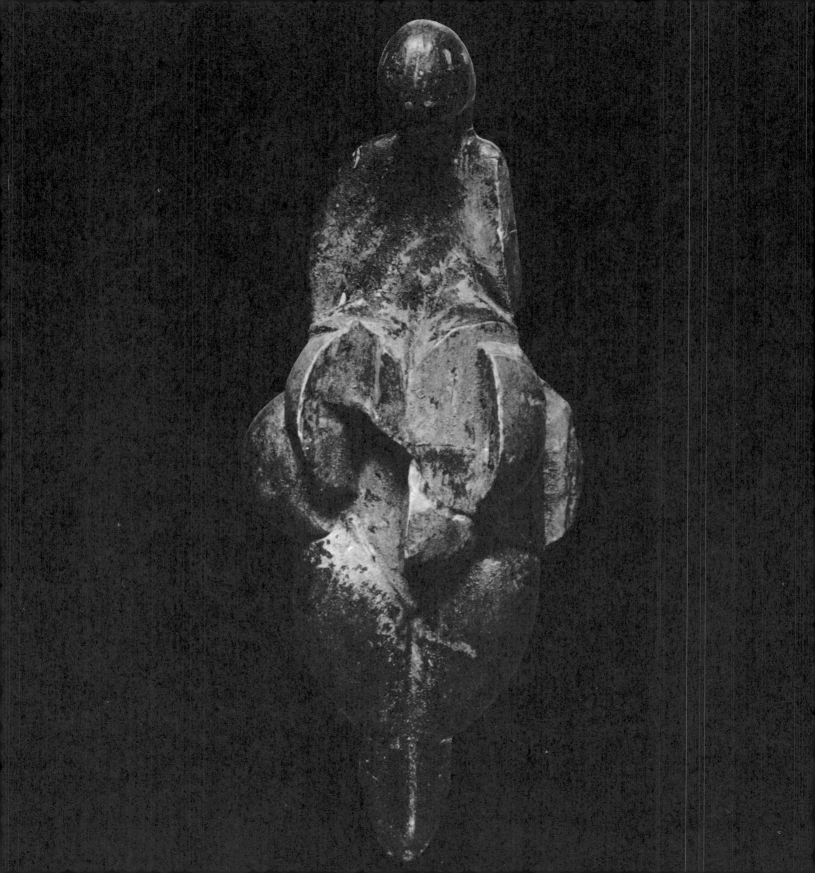

The images which make up this group of representations of the human body encompass a time span of approximately fifty thousand years. We have for that long been at work at making our own image. It is hard to decide which is more remarkable: that man has the capacity, or that he has the desire to do so.

Perhaps both are part of the same thing, the drive of the human being to be human. Obviously, none of these figures gives, or even aspires to, an individual likeness. In fact, none represent the human body "as it really is." We are not introduced here to Mrs. X or Mr. Y. These are not portraits. The ladies and gentlemen, so unmistakably endowed with the characteristics of our own bodies, are symbols. They are carriers, or vessels, of significance beyond themselves. They embody the dimensions of man's experience (rather than merely his appearance) which is polarized as divine power, as ancestral presence, as (pro-) creative essence.

The four-armed Shiva, the many-breasted Artemis, incorporate psychological realities—and how gallantly is the physical reality modified to serve them! Likewise, all of the images make use of the human figure not for its own sake, but to serve the process of man's self-identification.

The stone block from which the Venus was carved formed the center of a sanctuary, probably a fertility shrine. Also referred to as the "woman with the horn." Venus of Laussel. Limestone, C. 18" high. Discovered in a cave near Laussel, Dordogne, S. France. Solutrean period, C. 40,000 B.C. (Musée de l'Homme, Paris. Photo by Achille Weider.)

The essential body features are condensed into images which represent the male and female principles.
Violin-shaped female idol. Marble, a few inches high. Island of Amoyos in the Cyclades. C. 2500 B.C. (Ashmolean Museum, Oxford.)

Opposite: Castor and Pollux were the twin sons of Leda, whom Zeus had visited in the guise of a swan. Never has a male body looked like the one of this demigod; but so powerful has been the Greek vision of it that it has to this day conditioned ours.
Castor, the Divine Twin. Marble. Roman theater at Leptis Magna, North Africa. Second century A.D. (Photo by Roloff Beny.)

Door panel from a granary. Wood, with carving in relief. 62 cm. high. Dogon tribe. Mali, Western Sudan. (Rietberg Museum, Zurich.)

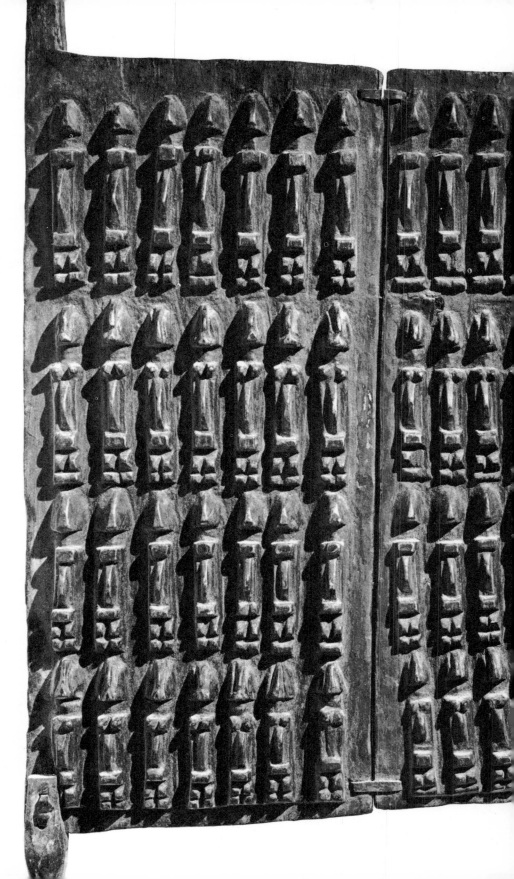

60

Artemis Ephesia   African   Mexican Tlazolteotl   Cranach: "Paradise"
                    Goddess   (Garden of Eden)

Artemis and the African and Mexican goddesses protect fertility and childbirth. The ancestors at the gate keep watch over the generations. Procreation is the only salvation; that is, it ensures immortality, survival beyond one's own death. In Cranach's representation of the "Garden of Eden" another message is incorporated: a creator calls man into being once and for all.

The breasts of this mother figure seem to be able to nurse everlastingly. Childless women seek her help. The headdress has the shape of an ostrich, which, as it lays many eggs, is a symbol of fertility to the Senufo. Fertility Statue with Twins. Wood, 65 cm. high. Senufo tribe, Ivory Coast, West Africa. (Rietberg Museum, Zurich.)

Opposite: Tlazolteotl, goddess of birth and procreation, shown giving birth to Centeotl, the maize god, or to Xochiquetzal, goddess of flowers, Patron of Souls. Tlazolteotl. Aztec Goddess. Stone, 20.5 cm. high. Fifteenth/sixteenth century. (Robert Woods Bliss Collection. National Gallery of Art, Washington, D.C.)

63

Eve was made from Adam's rib; the Buddha sprang from his mother's side. Ideas about creation resemble each other around the world. The Western and the Far Eastern version of man's separation from the world of nature are close—man and tree are severed entities—as compared to the tree-fern figure, where human and natural being are of one piece.

Left: Lucas Cranach the Elder: "Adam and Eve in the Garden of Eden." Oil. 1530. (Kunsthistorisches Museum, Vienna.)

Right: Ancestral Figure on Pole. Tree fern, total height 74". Gaua, New Hebrides. (Museum für Völkerkunde, Basle.)

The god who "sets everything in motion" pivots on his right foot, unfolds his limbs upward like a spreading tree. He revolves around his own axis, which is also the axis of the universe.

Dancing Shiva (Nataraja). Bronze, South India. Eighteenth/nineteenth century (from a form conceived in the eleventh century). (Collection of the Philadelphia Museum of Art.)

Ancestral Figure

Shiva rests in eternal motion, virtually containing all opposing directions; the stillness arises from the perfect balance of opposites in counterbalancing vibration. St. George's ballet with the dragon: the combat of aggressive Western dualism.

Above and overleaf: The armored knight is a universal image, shared by different cultures in different forms. The virgin assists the fighter through her presence. On her side the earth is tilled, an orderly garden; on his side it is wild, dark, and exposed.
Paolo Uccello: "St. George and the Dragon." Fifteenth century. Oil. (Musée Jacquemart-André, Paris.)

Above: The figure, at once sensuous and radiant, is seated in the gesture of instruction on the lotus flower.
Buddha. Bronze. Java, Indonesia. Eighth/ninth century A.D. (Collection Dr. and Mrs. Samuel Eilenberg.)

Right: Another gesture of instruction. The body of the enthroned Saviour is all but absorbed by the elaborately swirling folds of his robe.
"Christ in Majesty." Ivory plate on the cover of the Gospels. Carolingian, ninth/tenth century. (Staatl. Museen, Berlin.)

Three similar hands from representations of different "instructors"; God the Father, Buddha, and Christ. Each gesture has a different meaning. See also the hands of Shiva on pages 66–67.

Below: The artist's veneration is matched by his interest in a bravura feat of foreshortening. A human corpse, viewed in steep perspective, is composed within the geometry of a pentagon.
Andrea Mantegna: "Dead Christ." Oil. End of fifteenth century. (Brera Gallery, Milan.)

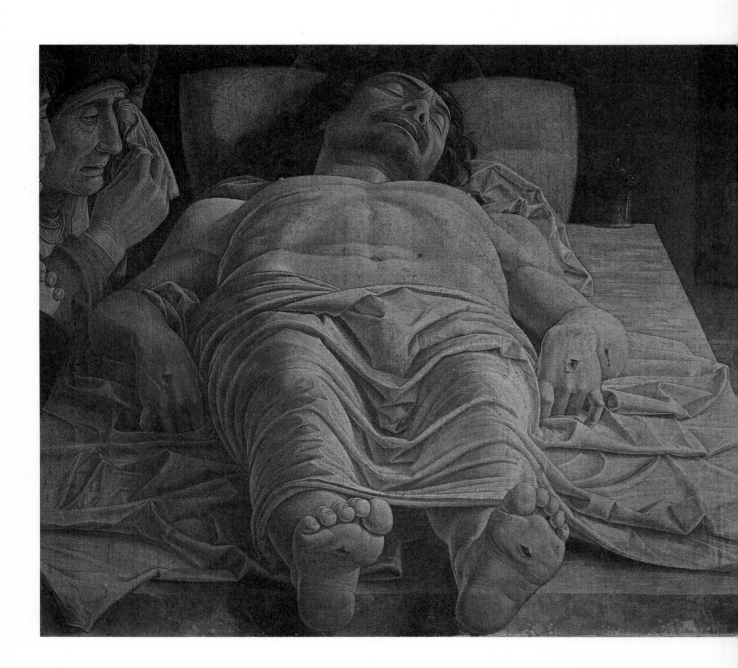

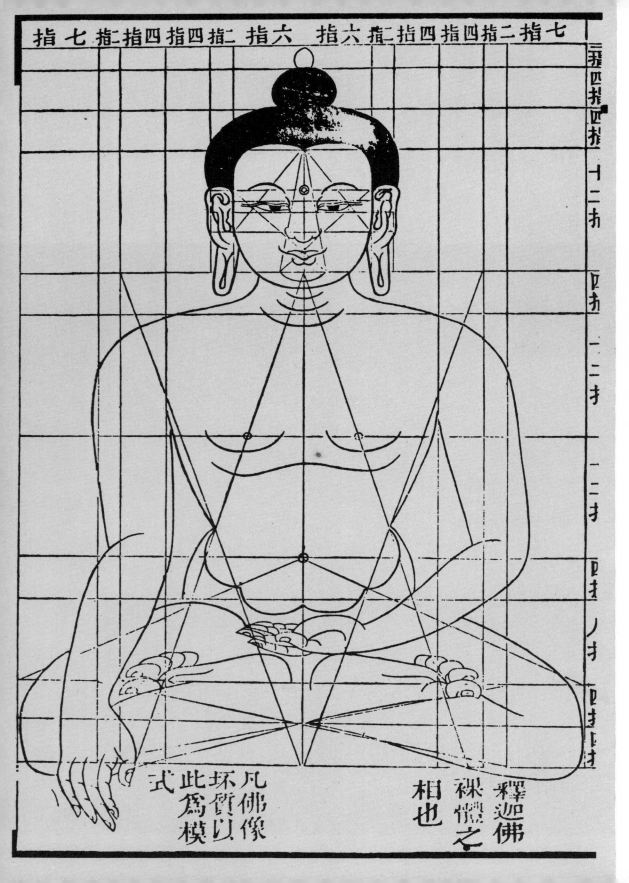

指七指二指四指四指二指六　指六指二指四指四指二指七

二指四指四指　十二指　四指　十二指　一二指　一二指　四指　八指　四指指

凡佛像以　壞質以　此為模式

釋迦佛　裸體之　相也

Both East and West worked out systems of relationships for the human figure which had more to do with an ultimate harmony of proportions than with the natural measurements of the body.

Left: Canon of Buddhist iconography. Eighteenth century, China. (Rijksmuseum voor Volkenkunde, Leiden.)

Opposite: Leonardo da Vinci: "Vitruvian Man." Fifteenth Century. (Galleria dell'Accademia, Venice.)

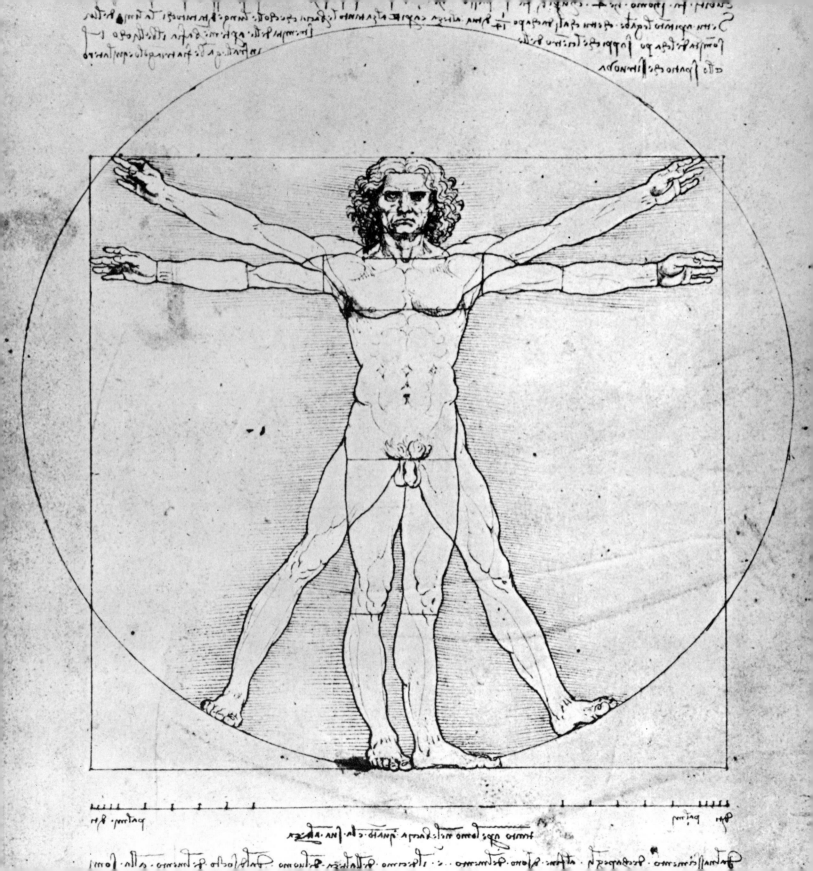

The human representations on this and the following pages are descriptive. The artists record definite situations, particular conditions, and specific individuals. They also inform us about a specific location or event, the time of year, and the social standing and age of the subject. In most cases we also know the names of the artists and when and where they lived.

We are witnessing here a pictorial record of man's discovery of the empirical world and, perhaps more importantly, that he has learned to master that world. In the last few hundred years the eyes of all of us have been educated in this tradition. We are insatiably fascinated with the world of appearances, with the world "as it is." This same fascination produces the inquisitiveness of science.

Around the turn of this century, art—which reveals man to his own understanding—took a different direction. The human image "disappears," as it were; it merges with its environment. At the same time, in the work of other artists, the human image reappears, but no longer as a particular person at a particular place or event.

Everything in this fabric of life is meant to be read symbolically as well as literally. The human figure is more of a "signpost" (standing for virginity) than an individual.
"The Lady and the Unicorn" *(La Dame à la Licorne)*. 1499. One in a series of five tapestries. (Musée de Cluny, Paris.)

The tapestry, "The Lady and the Unicorn," is filled with many meaning-
ful details, each contributing to the total medieval presence of the
world in which the lady here is an integral part.

In contrast, Bronzino's portrait, at right, concentrates on the individual,
a man obviously conscious of himself and of his identity as a man.
In the second version of Matisse's "Sailor" the heraldic quality that
resided in the adornments around the medieval figure reasserts itself,
but it is now property of the figural form itself. A further transition is
evident in the work of Van Gogh, who, with acute self-awareness,
painted the portrait of his inner self (page 79).

Left: The proud restraint and self-awareness of the young man is matched by that of the artist. Bronzino: "Portrait of a Young Man." Oil. Middle of the sixteenth century. (The Metropolitan Museum of Art, Bequest of Mrs. H. O. Havemeyer, 1929. The H. O. Havemeyer Collection.)

Within one year's time the artist changes the meaning of the same subject. He shifts the emphasis from an individual likeness of his son to a generalized emblematic image of any young sailor. See also overleaf.
Henri Matisse: "Young Sailor." Oil. 1905. "Young Sailor." Oil. 1906. (Collection of Mr. and Mrs. Leigh B. Block, Chicago.)

With men such as Gabo or Giacometti, artists once again begin to make symbolic statements about the human condition in general. In so doing they show our dilemma: that the time of acute self-awareness of the human being as an individual is also the time when our sense of identity is most in jeopardy.

Right: The human body is understood in terms of the relationships between its members. A "constellation" of and within the body is highlighted,

and the light streaming over it is part of the sculpture.
Auguste Rodin: "Crouching Woman." Bronze. 1882. (Rodin Museum, Paris.)

Above: The artist as an individual, the individual as an artist, faces himself, alone, with anxious scrutiny.
Vincent Van Gogh: "Self-portrait." Oil. 1890. (The Louvre, Paris.)

Images of the "headaches" of our own time, of our self-conscious awareness, which is challenged by the technological world—which we ourselves created.
Opposite: Naum Gabo. Bust. Plastic. 1916. (Gemeente Museum, Amsterdam.)
Above: Raoul Hausmann: "Mechanical Head," also called "The Spirit of Our Time." Wood and various other materials. 1919. (Collection of the artist.)

Below: For a devotional book, this is a very worldly representation of the spring season. Nature is discovered, along with the pleasures of everyday life.

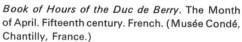

Book of Hours of the Duc de Berry. The Month of April. Fifteenth century. French. (Musée Condé, Chantilly, France.)

Right: A moment as fleeting as the sunlight flickers on the garden path holds a social and a seasonal situation—both in bloom. The white dresses of the ladies float fluffily through the foliage like so many showers of blossoms.
Claude Monet: "Women in the Garden." Oil. 1866–67. (The Louvre, Paris.)

Strollers on the borders of the Seine are subjected to the most intricate geometry of formal and rhythmic relationships. The little girl in white (just off center) functions as the prism for the color refraction throughout the picture.

Georges Seurat: "An Afternoon at La Grande Jatte." Oil. 1884. (The Metropolitan Museum of Art, Bequest of Samuel A. Lewisohn, 1951.)

The figures become part of the park; they blend into it as though they were trees. Both serve in a structure of color intensities.
August Macke: "Strollers at the Blue Lake." Oil. 1914. (Staatliche Kunsthalle, Karlsruhe, Germany.)

The uprising of the masses is captured and focused in this scene of the Napoleonic wars. The central figure, in blazing yellows and whites, seems to be aflame, illuminating the surrounding darkness like a signal-fire.
Francisco Goya: "The Shootings of May 3rd, 1808 at Madrid." Oil. 1814. (The Prado, Madrid.)

Opposite: A new version of a symbolic rather than naturalistic view of man. Among the characteristics: weightlessness, visibility of the whole of the body; and overemphasized sense organs as receptacles of world experience.
Pablo Picasso: *"Les Demoiselles d'Avignon."* Oil. 1907. (Collection, The Museum of Modern Art, New York. Acquired through the Lillie P. Bliss Bequest.)

A majestic pyramid, glistening and transparent, is built of groups of women and trees. Secular nymphets hold up the sky with which they have merged.
Paul Cézanne: *"The Large Bathers."* Oil. 1898–1905. (Philadelphia Museum of Art: W. P. Wilstach Collection.)

Opposite: For Léger, human bodies and machines were equally organic. He saw them both as part of one and the same human vitality and creativeness.

Fernand Léger: "Three Women" *(Le grand déjeuner).* Oil. 1921. (Collection, The Museum of Modern Art, New York. Mrs. Simon Guggenheim Fund.)

The human body participates in its environment. It is a landscape itself, permeable and mutable, with valleys and ridges, cavities and peaks.

Henry Moore: "Recumbent Figure." Stone. 1938–39. (The Tate Gallery, London.)

The polarity of two entities in one is stated and mastered through a geometric structure of forms, at once imaginative and strict.

Henri Matisse: "Two Negresses." Bronze. 1908. (The Joseph H. Hirshhorn Collection.)

Opposite: The figures are overstretched in solitariness, pinpointed in space by tension. While the group resembles a forest, and seems that anonymous, it also defines a state of being.

Alberto Giacometti: "Square, Seven Figures and One Head." Bronze. 1950. (The Readers Digest Association.)

Mouth and navel are fused into a mouthpiece in the center of this head-torso. The seer's legs are fused with his seat; his brow has the suggestion of a headgear— under which the gaze must be far-reaching.

Kenneth Armitage: "Prophet 1961." Bronze. 1961. (Marlborough Fine Art, London.)

Opposite: The essence of femininity is a timeless topic in the human endeavor to understand, as well as to acknowledge and praise creation. Human efforts, since prehistoric times, echo through these figures.

James Rosati: "Undine." Marble. 1959–60. (Courtesy of the artist.)

The representations of human figures assembled here are by artists who are, without exception, our contemporaries. All of them were born within this century.

Also without exception, these artists are not seeking to describe, or to make likenesses of, specific persons. They follow and develop the direction toward symbolic image making which artistic expression assumed around the turn of this century.

We are no longer presented with individuals, but with "types," such as "the" prophet, "the" usurper, "the" earth, or feminine essence and fecundity. These works seem to come close to the earliest representations of man by man. Yet there is, naturally and inevitably, a difference. The prehistoric documents of our existence are oriented toward the cosmos; that is, they beseech the unknown "out there," as it were, and represent it in the form of divinities and idols. On the other hand, the record we make of ourselves, in the present, is man-centered.

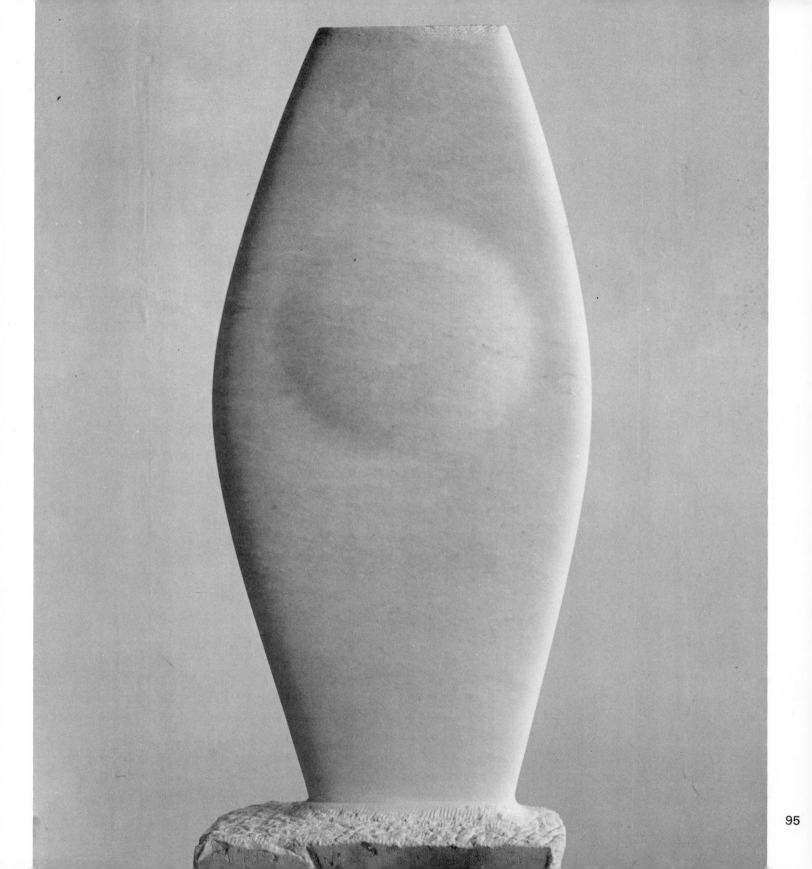

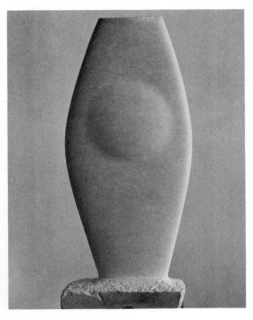

James Rosati: "Undine." 1959–60.

Kenneth Armitage: "Prophet." 1961.

Hans Aeschbacher: "Female Figure." Marble. 1949. (Courtesy of the artist.)

Jean Dubuffet: "Portrait Combouis." Heavy impasto on canvas. 1945. (Pierre Matisse Gallery, New York.)

Opposite: This is, perhaps, another Earth Mother. The human being merges with the earth it is made of, and the human being emerges and grows from the earth in the quest for its identity.

Jean Ipousteguy: *La Terre.* Plaster. 1962. (Pierre Matisse Gallery, New York.)

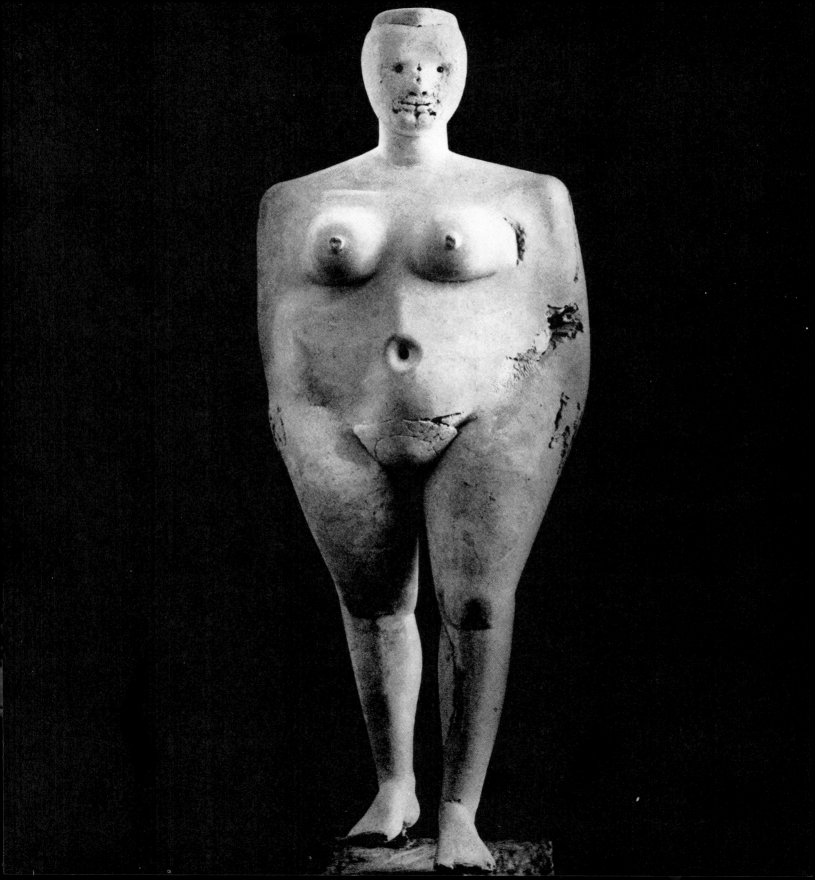

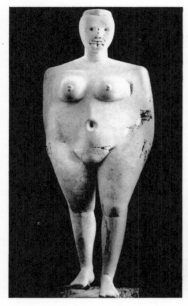

Ipoustegy: "La Terre."

de Kooning: "Woman IV."

Our human images today are symbols also, but their orbit and frame of reference is man, here and now. We have actually, physically, reached the "out there"; outer space is becoming a measurable and populated place. This makes man, his place and stature in the world, more important as well as less important: he is in control of his environment, he is absorbed by it, but at times he is smothered by it.

Although the ancient mythical quality is evoked, Adam and Eve are a man and a woman of our own flesh.
Nora Speyer: "The Expulsion." Oil. 1964. (Courtesy of the artist.)

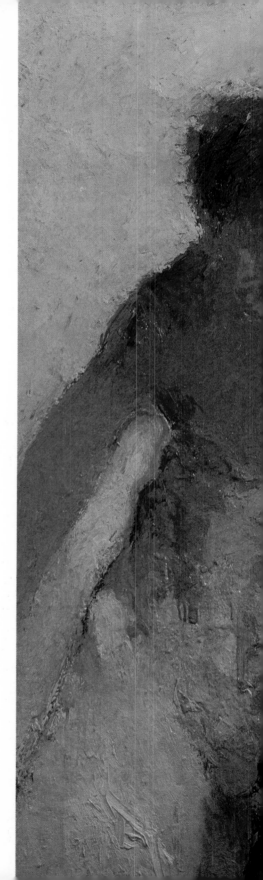

An inner likeness is portrayed which informs the outer features. These are captured as a sparse script of signs, articulating the open space of which we are a part.

Alice Yamin: "Marlene." Carbon. 1962. (Lida Moser, New York.)

Opposite page: The figure spreads over the whole of the picture surface. It encompasses and constitutes the landscape of human experience.

Willem de Kooning: "Woman IV." Oil. 1952–53. (Nelson Gallery—Atkins Museum. Gift of Mr. William Inge.)

An attempt at a contemporary form of portraiture: individual features are enlarged and highly stylized, so that they shed their individuality. A comment on the billboard civilization.
Alex Katz: "Smile Again." Oil. 1965. (Courtesy, Fischbach Gallery.)

Out of the dark, a luminous body bursts forth still covered with the shreds of chaos. A modern birth of the ancient Venus who arose from the foam of the sea.
Nicholas Marsicano: "She." Oil. 1959. (Collection, The Museum of Modern Art, New York. Gift of Larry Aldrich.)

American scene "jazzed up" blends with the smolderingly serious issue, Black and White, in this bright, melancholy, and ironic apparition.
Richard Lindner: "Moon over Alabama." Oil. 1963. (Mr. and Mrs. Charles B. Benenson.)

Elements of the junkyard are rescued—to become elegant. The comment on our world is in
the materials used as well as in what they
have become.
Richard Stankiewicz: "Beach Sitter." 1958.
(Courtesy of the artist.)

Humor and wit are elements not only of this
sculpture, but of other works in this volume.
Overblown forms (windblown sails of iron)
evoke the idea of pomposity and unstable
balance.
Robert Mueller: "The Usurper." Iron. 1959.
(Permission A.D.A.G.P. 1967 by French
Reproduction Rights, Inc.)

A conglomerate of disparate parts is welded into a symbolic image of human existence—at once heroic and ridiculous.

Roel d'Haese: "Legendary Personage." Bronze. 1956. (Collection Benedict Goldschmidt, Brussels.)

The German title is a pun; it can mean "Larkspur" as well as "Knight's Spur," connoting the frailty of man as well as his aggressiveness. Man and his armor are indivisible.

Robert Mueller: "Rittersporn." Iron. 1958. (Joseph H. Hirshhorn Collection.)

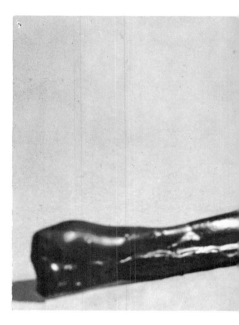

Left: Even if we appear to be self-contained pillars of strength, we are full of complexities and hidden forces which intercommunicate and are at cross purposes.

Marisol: "The Blacks." Wood. 1961–62. (Collection Eleanor Ward.)

The human figure becomes a landscape, and a harbor is translated into a welcoming feminine embrace.

George Spaventa: "Harbor." Bronze. 1963. (Poindexter Gallery.)

This figure is composed of ten independent metal pieces which interlock. It conjures up human power contained, human power forcefully wielded, intensely bundled, shining and moving.

Miguel Berrocal: "Samson." Chromed bronze. 1963. (Private collection.)

MEANS
COLOR — OBJECTS — SPACE

Opposite: A guardian presence: the oval of the face is articulated, and its features are summed up, if not over-ruled, by the power of the color shapes.

Ridge piece; gable decoration: polychrome face. From the Sepik Valley, New Guinea. (The American Museum of Natural History, New York.)

The artist, as the spokesman for his kind, is forever dealing with the world of phenomena, with reality, which he seeks to transcend in the process. In this way, man has produced and has left us a faithful record of his adventures: works of art tell what they are and what they mean. The foregoing chapter explored this with examples of the human likeness, the procession and the human appearances speaking eloquently for themselves. While the subject remained the same, interpretation changed according to what man looked like and meant to himself at various times and in various places.

This last chapter is concerned with the means at the artist's disposal. These means (not to be confused with the media, i.e., techniques and skills, such as etching) have been the same ever since man ventured into the hazards of image making. The "data" are inescapable—there is always light to deal with, and correlated with it shadow and color, or their absence; there is always form, and correlated with it volume and delineation; there is always space, and correlated with it location, structure, definition of place and scale. Without these elements, no formal order is possible; with them, formal order *is* possible.

Strong and definite limitations in the nature and essence of formal endeavor compel the image makers to be imaginative—limitlessly so—in the handling of their means.

Details from page 110.

Uniform, unmodeled color areas pull the human face and body beyond their "natural" boundaries. The lady "communicates with her environment," she "flows over": she gives a lecture.

Paul Klee: "Omphalo-centric Lecture." Paste color on silk, glued onto jute. 1939. (Kunstsammlung, Nordrhein-Westfalen, Düsseldorf, Germany.)

Several people are involved with each other. Their bodily extensions overlap, interpenetrate. One and the same color area is a location with different meanings, according to the context in which it is read. One person's kidney is another's cheek.

Joan Miró: "Inverse Personages." Oil. 1949. (Kunstmuseum, Basle, Switzerland.)

In this blend of container and human body, a decorative geometric pattern is carried through undeviatingly. By disregarding or overwhelming the human features, it emphasizes them.

Figure vessel of painted clay: a man asleep wearing a patterned garment and large earplugs. Moche culture, Peru. (Collection of Dr. Bernoulli, Basle, Switzerland.)

The sensation of vertigo is captured dramatically; bodies and limbs are multiplied, fragmented, and scattered.

Colors have shaken loose from their objects and float around separately, as independent elements.

Fernand Léger: *Les Deux Acrobates*. Oil. 1942–43. (Courtesy Sidney Janis Gallery, New York.)

The blue color functions as an over-all envelope, as a revealing and, at the same time, concealing garment. While it shows the figure, it also makes it inaccessible.

Detail of standing figure. Wood, drenched in washing-blue. New Hebrides Islands. (Musée de l'Homme, Paris.)

Light, or rather the absence of light, namely shadow, is rendered by means of blue color. In "reality," the lady wears a white dress. The intense ex-

perience thus transmitted: the coolness of the shade on a hot summer day. Georges Seurat: "Lady with the Parasol." Oil. 1884—85. (Collection Bührle, Zurich, Switzerland.)

Below: The artist joins different planes into one plane, the picture surface, by using the same blue for the sky and for the garb of the saint. It is as though the sky blue were funneled into the central figure, filling it with heavenly substance. Giotto: "St. Francis Gives His Cloak to a Beggar." (Fresco, Basilica of St. Francis in Assisi. 1296.)

Below right: Basically the same thing is happening as in the Giotto. The blue areas pull different depths into the same picture plane. Shadows are translated into pools of blue color. Instead of creating depth, they destroy it. Wassily Kandinsky: "Murnau." Oil. 1909. (Collection of Prof. Kurt Martin, Munich.) *Above:* Shades of blue become structured "fields," and arrive at a subtly tuned spatial landscape by means of planes differently shaded, joined, and tautly stretched. Ludwig Sander: "Chinook I." Oil. 1965. (Collection of Wynant D. Vanderpool.)

In both these pictures the image is divided along a middle axis by the arrangement of juxtaposed—cool and warm—color areas. Solid flat color planes speak as strongly as the body features which they all but dissolve or absorb.

Henri Matisse: "Madame Matisse/Portrait with Green Stripe." Oil. 1905. (The Royal Museum of Fine Arts, Copenhagen. J. Rump Collection.)

The Madonna of Tolga. Fourteenth century. Icon of the Jaroslavl School.

Although the symbolic use of red (on the dress) and blue (on the coat) for the Madonna is maintained, the artist's major effort is to make the viewer forget color, to make color incidental and subservient to a faithful rendering of a mother with child.

Gheerardt David: "Virgin with Child at the Breast." Early sixteenth century. (Museo Lazaro Galdiano, Madrid.)

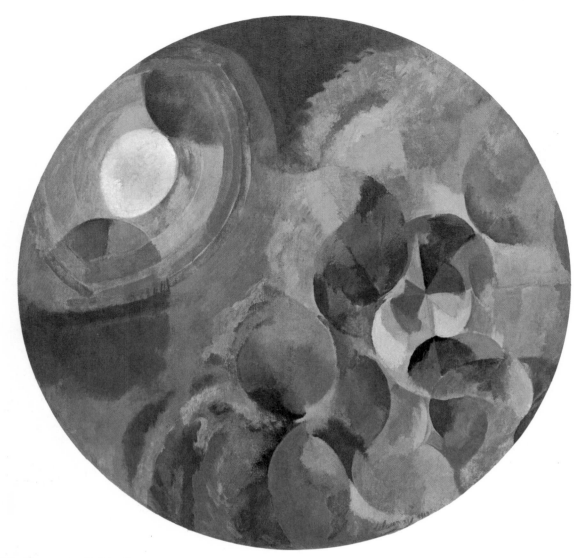

The bursting of light into the spectrum colors glorifies the sky-night and earth-day in an image of revolving movements reminiscent of stellar orbits. A painter-poet's vision before man experienced outer space. Robert Delaunay: "Sun Disks." Oil. 1912–13. (Collection, The Museum of Modern Art, New York. Mrs. Simon Guggenheim Fund.)

Color and light

Color is not just color. It is not just a matter of setting red down in one place on a surface and blue in another, or of knowing how one color can affect the presence and quality of another simply by being its neighbor. These are matters of skill, professional experience, and mastery.

There is really no such thing as "beautiful colors" in painting, or, at any rate, colors are not, in themselves, sufficient to sustain a painting as a work of art. Color must be connected with a structural order.

In the first group of paintings in this section, color is given structural quality and function (see pages 107, 108–109). Uniform color surfaces assume an independent role; they become a formal element in themselves. Forms consisting of nothing but a blue or red compete and overlap with "straight" forms such as body features.

In the second selection, on pages 110–111, uses of blue for different purposes connect the pictures within each group— blue to create distance (Giotto) or to close it out (Kandinsky); blue to depict a blue garment (Giotto) as opposed to blue to depict a shadow on a white dress (Seurat).

Color is always used to serve the dynamic architecture of a work, even in the most evanescent-looking one. Were it not for the rigorous structure underlying the picture by Rothko (page 119), it would not be able to project its intensity.

Observation of the rainbow serves to represent the other-worldly light of revelation. Matthias Grünewald: "The Resurrection." Oil on wood. 1515. (Detail from the Isenheim Altar in Colmar.)

Opposite: Once again the rainbow colors manifest a state of luminosity. The appearance world in the sunset afterglow reverberates light as color, and the retina registers color as light.
André Derain: "Charing Cross Bridge." Oil. 1905–1906. (Private Collection, New York.)

Right: The presence of light, majestic and austere, detached from a particular incidence. Color is turned into sheer radiance. It is as though white heat were steaming from the intense red glow.
Mark Rothko: "Number 8." Oil. 1952. (Collection of Mr. and Mrs. Burton Tremaine, Meriden, Conn.)

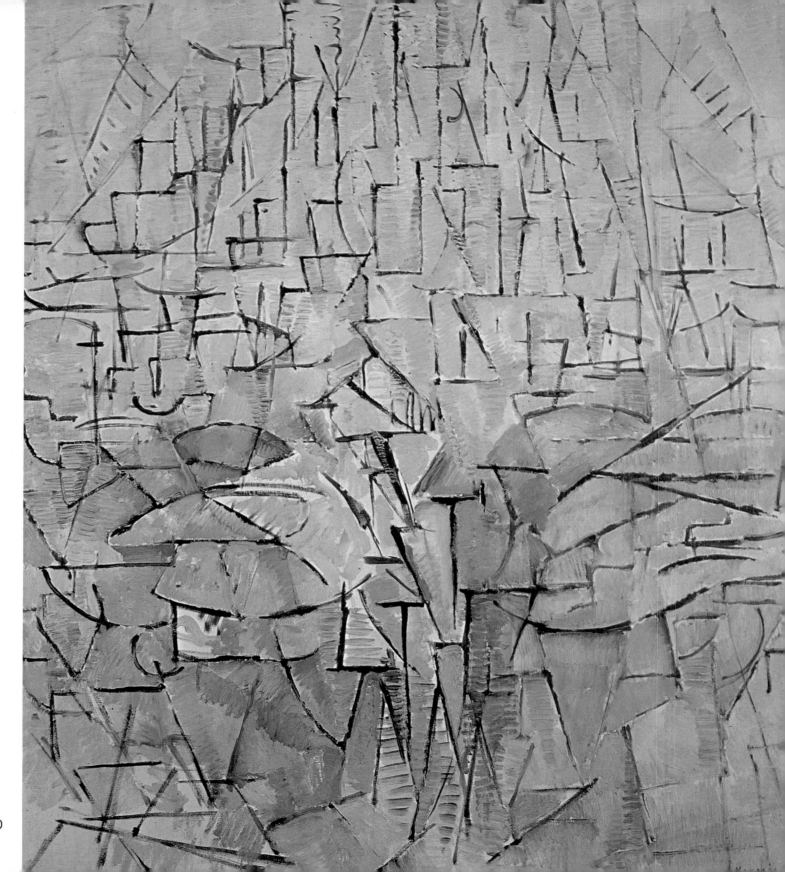

Opposite: The artist's overriding interest in structure, and in making its workings apparent, reduces the use of color to the barest necessity. The resulting transparency yields up a kind of sparse illumination from within the picture.
Piet Mondrian: "Composition 3" (Trees). Oil. *C.* 1912. (Collection S. B. Slijper, The Hague.)

Right: The material substance or "object-ness" of the cathedral is submerged and dissolved in light. Color is compelled to render the flickering atmosphere.
The density of the stone "disappears" in luminosity.
Claude Monet: "Rouen Cathedral, the Façade at Sunset." Oil. 1894. (Museum of Fine Arts, Boston. Juliana Cheney Edwards Collection.)

Objects

These pictures have been selected with the idea of exploring the role which the world of objects has played in the world of art. It is generally believed that it is the aim and purpose of art to render as closely as possible the object world or "things as they are." This is, quite simply, not true. It seems to have been true for a comparatively limited period of time in our own Western culture (for the three to four hundred years from the Renaissance to the middle of the nineteenth century). Yet what makes those pictures works of art is certainly not the fruit bowl. Artists have been and are concerned with interests beyond the representation of reality "as it is," even though all of them (be they Bushmen or Yale men, Spaniards or Congolese) have loved and used that reality, and love it and make use of it today.

There is reality and there is our experience of reality. The artist reveals them both. He does not imitate reality, he matches it.

Double Hooks,
see overleaf.

Opposite and right: The wearer of this object is not only protected by the shielding metal but also by the half-human, half-crested alligator deity worked into it. Golden breast-plate. Pre-Columbian. Sitio Conte, Cocle Province, Panama. (Andre Emmerich, Inc.)

The blade is of iron, while strips of copper are wound around the shaft. It is decorated with the image of the mother of the tribe. When the king appears in public he carries a small ax such as this on his shoulder as an emblem of his royal power.
Ceremonial ax. Wood. Baluba-bahemba tribe, S. E. Congo. (Rietberg Museum, Zurich.)

There are periods in man's existence when there is no art. That is, there is no desire or necessity to make objects with no other purpose and intention but to become "art". The artists, at such times, are monks, ship-builders, medicine men, masons, carvers, potters, who are highly skilled craftsmen and who have been trained to implore the favors of gods and ancestors to come to dwell in their artifacts, to invest the powers, draw them into the artful patterns which the gods taught them in the first place. They are skilled in re-enacting the patterns or codes designed to channel the presence of the powers into everyday life and objects.

So everything is made as beautifully and skillfully as possible, and the workaday objects have the quality of what we would call art. The container, double-hooks, and ceremonial ax are such objects. They serve a life which is ceremonial throughout, in the most humble and simple activities.

Left: Ancestral guardians watch what is hooked on to their feet. They are fastened, free-hanging, to the roof inside the hut. Baskets of food, hunks of meat, and trophies such as enemy heads are hung on them to protect these possessions from rodents.
Two double-hook boards. Carved and painted wood. The beard of

the figure on the right is made of human hair. Sepik, New Guinea. (Sammlung für Völkerkunde, Zurich University; Musée d'Ethnographie, Neuchâtel.)

Above: The interest in making a container and a bird are identical. The sense of direction strongly asserted in the right-angular arrangement of beak, handle, and tail appears to have oriented it in the four directions of the universe. Bird Effigy Vessel. Red pottery with cream decoration. 6¾" long, 6" high. Mochica. North coast of Peru. *C.* 300 B.C.—100 A.D. (Courtesy Emmerich Gallery, New York.)

The virgin's purity is symbolized by the white lily. A symbolic meaning of virginity is also attached to the tidy garden enclosure.

Rogier van der Weyden: "The Annunciation." Tempera and oil on wood. *C.* 1400–1464. (The Metropolitan Museum of Art, Gift of J. Pierpont Morgan, 1917.)

Opposite: There is a hinged cover on the top of the dove's body, and the Host is placed inside. Originally a wider plate was attached to the bottom. It was suspended by a series of chains over the altar. The wings of the dove are movable.

Eucharistic dove, Limoges. Champlevé enamel on copper-gilt. Thirteenth century. (The Metropolitan Museum of Art, the Cloisters Collection, Purchase, 1947.)

Double Hooks

v. d. Weyden: "Annunciation."

Cranach: "Adam and Eve."

When an object has symbolic quality, it inevitably participates in situations of mediation and exchange. When the dove stands for the Holy Ghost, a balance for the weighing of the human soul, a shift of power changes or closes a situation, creating a dialogue. Such activities cease to occur as soon as the symbolic world which they express ceases to exist. Suddenly, there is no longer any "partner" for the lonesome woman in "After the Meal," almost smothered by her surroundings, and not, like "The Lady with the Unicorn," enhanced by them. This happens after the transaction in the "Payment" has become profane and reasonable. The human figure eventually disappears altogether. The fruit bowl in front of her takes the stage and it, in turn, is replaced by the interest in forms and volumes in space. (See pages 132–133.)

There is no interest in the scale as such, as an object, except as an instrument of justice. The merit of a cause is weighed to determine a mortal's fate. "Judgment." Detail from an altar piece. Painted wood panel. Catalonia, Spain. (Museo Diocesano, Vich.)

The apple still has symbolic significance; so do the snake, the vine, which stands for the coming Saviour, and the stork. But the end of Paradise is also the beginning of the terrestrial —and empirical—world, and of man's taking possession thereof.
Lucas Cranach the Elder: "Adam and Eve." Oil on wood. 1526. (Courtauld Institute Galleries, London.)

Opposite: A worldly, profane scene, and an utterly secularized object world! Pomegranate and grapes appear on the table, so do bread and wine—devoid of symbolic meaning and enjoyed, with gusto, for their own sakes.
Lucas Cranach the Elder: "The Payment." Oil on wood. 1532. (National Museum, Stockholm.)

To Cranach (left) the fruit has symbolic meaning; its significance derives as much from the fact that it is the forbidden fruit as from its being a wonderful fruit. For Zurbaran (right) the object is simply a fruit—wonderful, delectable. To Matisse and Cézanne (below and opposite page) fruits cease to be fruits, and become forms, volumes in space. In the Cézanne the fruits look as artificial as the plates and the cloth on which they are arranged. The artist's interest is concentrated on how one object is at once distinct, yet bound up with another adjacent to it. In the Matisse chair, fruit, and woman are engulfed by the crimson color which establishes a field for formal relations. The same garland design in cloth and wallpaper unites foreground and background into one realm.

Left: Francisco Zurbarán: "Still Life." Oil. C. 1633. (Count Contini Bonacossi, Florence.)

Opposite page, bottom: Henri Matisse: "After the Meal" *(La desserte rouge).* Oil. 1908. (Hermitage Museum, Leningrad, Russia.)

Below: Paul Cézanne: "Apples and Oranges." Oil. 1895–1900. (Louvre, Paris.)

The fur is carefully, even tenderly, fitted. The feeling of sensuousness clashes with the expectation of drinking. A familiar object becomes unfamiliar, if not revolting; it is shifted into the dimension from which dreams come.
Meret Oppenheim: "Object." Fur-covered cup, saucer, and spoon. 1936. (Collection, The Museum of Modern Art, New York. Purchase.)

Everything about these objects, assembled into a new object, is incongruous. One would associate a bird with the cage—instead there is the conglomerate opacity of weight. The weight, in turn, has its temperature taken. There is method in the mystery, not only madness.
Marcel Duchamp: "Ready-Made, Why Not Sneeze Rose Selavy?" 1921. (Philadelphia Museum of Art.)

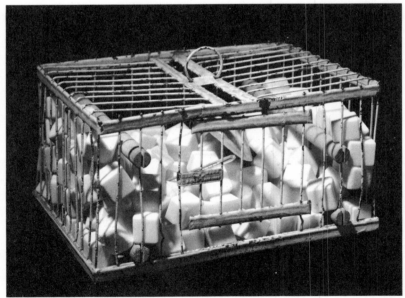

The animal has a round, bulky earthenware pot for a torso, and the toy car of the artist's son for a head. Objects are deprived of their identity and made part of a new object.
Pablo Picasso: "Baboon and Young." Bronze. 1951. (Collection, The Museum of Modern Art, New York. Mrs. Simon Guggenheim Fund.)

Opposite: A candle end, a wood shaving, and some boards suddenly are exempt from the perishable state because a poet has touched them and made them part of a form poem.
Kurt Schwitters: "Merz-Picture with Candle." Montage: mixed media on wood. 1925–28. (Marlborough Fine Art, London.)

After the world of "things" has left the realm of image making, it finds its clandestine return, so to speak, in the work of art becoming an object. They are compositions which combine oddments—randomly found pieces of junk, deliberately selected specimens of mass-produced anonymity—into units which emerge again as images: with no other purpose than that of being images and self-sufficient statements.

Below:
Prefabricated units—tubing produced for industrial use—perform an unexpected function: that of conveying the multitudinous scintillations of the night sky.
Zoltan Kemeny: "Milky Way." Yellow and red copper. 1954. (Collection World House Galleries, New York.)

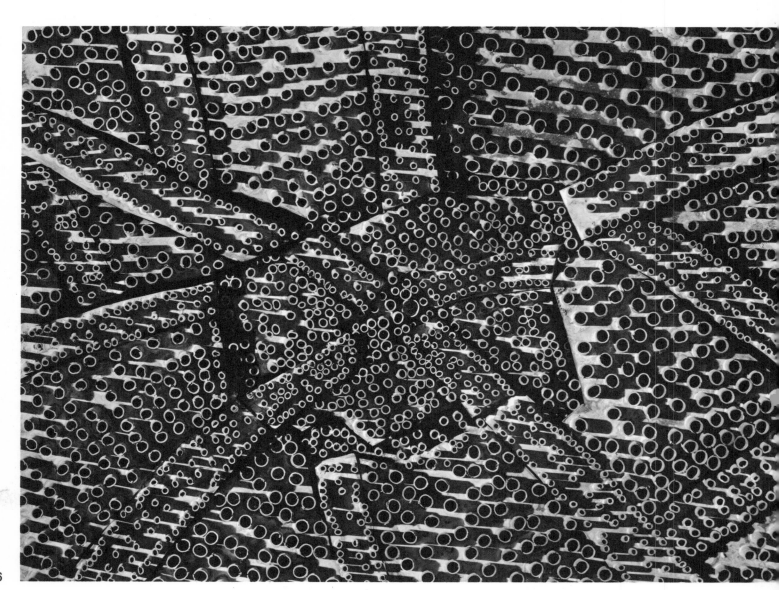

Left: A stuffed eagle, of American descent, pulled down by the fluffy weight of a pillow, flies below a pastiche of billboard paraphernalia. The city's rejects are resurrected into a new context of irony and insight. Robert Rauschenberg: "Canyon." 1959. Painting-combine. (Collection: Ileana Sonnabend.)

Below: Should the flag be mass-produced?
Jasper Johns: "3 Flags." Encaustic on canvas. 1958. (Collection Mr. and Mrs. Burton Tremaine, Meriden, Connecticut.)

Space

Gabo: "Linear Number 2." Detail.

Among the things that determine the character of a work of art is the spatial organization of the various elements contained in it. When we speak of space in painting or sculpture, we are talking about the creation and definition of a location or an environment, not only in the physical sense, but in the psychological sense as well. Awareness of space in life itself, and as artists achieve the feeling of space in a picture, is related to such basic questions as what distances (if any) we are called upon by the subject to travel, where we are being asked to travel, and at what speed. Relating ourselves to the world we know, we equate our own experience with the world the artist knows and has regarded as important enough to make visible to us.

It is customary to say that the Egyptians and the early Greeks did not know how to handle space and perspective. It would be more to the point to say that their interest in showing a man's body as completely and as explicitly as possible prevented them from inventing a method by which a shoulder or an arm might be omitted and the eye fooled into thinking it was there (page 149). The power of suggestion has—or should have—an important bearing on how the artist organizes his material. This is also true of perspective. If we examine the different positions of the spectator in relation to the sunset vistas on pages 144 and 145 we see in what sharp contrast our relationship is to these subjects and those shown on page 150. The space the latter represents is a "realm" in which processes of change are embedded, such as the growth of plant life under the waxing and waning phases of the moon or its decay under a black midnight sun.

Image making concerned with the
world of spiritual realities is
focused not on the spectator but
on itself. It is self-sufficient. The
encounter of two holy men can be
immersed in the infinite golden
ground of eternity.
"The Two Theodors." Oil on wood.
Ikon from northern Greece. Seven-
teenth century.

Opposite: Human life and activities are relevant in every detail, exciting and interesting as an experience. The world is a stage, with staggered sets, on which the daily human drama unfolds.
Ambrogio Lorenzetti: "Market Scene." One in a series of "allegories about the Results of Good and Bad Government" at the city hall of Siena. Middle of the fourteenth century. (Palazzo Pubblico, Siena, Italy.)

A virtuoso production in the handling of illusionistic space. The organization of the complex coil of limbs, human and equestrian, is incredibly skillful.
Peter Paul Rubens: "The Rape of the Daughters of Leukippus." Oil. 1618. (Alte Pinakothek, Munich, Germany.)

The endeavor is to condense the experience of depth into the two-dimensional picture plane. The sea and every element in the foreground lie at their full extension on the canvas surface.

Paul Cézanne: "The Gulf of Marseilles Seen from L'Estaque." Oil. 1883–85. (The Metropolitan Museum of Art, Bequest of Mrs. H. O. Havemeyer, 1929. The H. O. Havemeyer Collection. Photograph by Robert Crandall.)

Opposite: It is as though we were hovering inside a gigantic bowl. An eerie light throws the landscape into strangely exaggerated focus. The magic of the elements is summoned to symbolize human spectacle or divine majesty, or both.
Albrecht Altdorfer: "Detail of The Battle of Alexander." Oil. 1529. (Alte Pinakothek, Munich, Germany.)

Below: Claude Monet: Palazzo da Mula. Oil. 1908. (National Gallery of Art, Washington.)

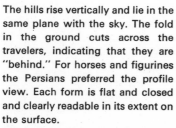

The hills rise vertically and lie in the same plane with the sky. The fold in the ground cuts across the travelers, indicating that they are "behind." For horses and figurines the Persians preferred the profile view. Each form is flat and closed and clearly readable in its extent on the surface.
Mihr and Mushtari of Assar: "Prince Mihr Cutting Off a Lion's Head at One Blow." Bukhara, 1523. (Courtesy of the Smithsonian Institution, Freer Gallery of Art, Washington, D.C.)

Right: The glory of an evening light emphasizes the thrust into the far distance. The small scale of the figures, the high sky above a low horizon; everything is designed to create the sensation of an immense expanse.
Claude Lorrain: "Cephalus and Procris Reunited by Diana." Oil. 1645. (Reproduced by courtesy of the Trustees, The National Gallery, London.)

Depth is dissolved in atmospheric mist. There is optical sensation and ephemeral reflection and counterreflection.

Claude Monet: "Palazzo da Mula, Venice." Oil. 1908. (National Gallery of Art, Washington, D.C., Chester Dale Collection.)

Opposite: The painter's perfect control of an interior space is subordinated to his keen and subtle interest in formal and color relationships.
Johannes Vermeer: "Girl Asleep." Oil. *C.* 1660. (The Metropolitan Museum of Art, Bequest of Benjamin Altman, 1913.)

Right: The desire for high visibility and clarity for the body features makes the idea of volume in depth appear negligible.
Relief in the tomb of Kha-em-het, Thebes. Amenophis III enthroned. Eighteenth Dynasty (*C.* 1400 B.C.). (Photograph by the Egyptian Expedition, The Metropolitan Museum of Art.)

Although the golden "background" is secularized, it assumes a similar function to the one found in Giotto's "Annunciation" above. The figure is ensconced in it, and volume yields to form; there is no room to sit.
Vincent Van Gogh: "L'Arlésienne" (Mme Ginoux). Oil. 1888. (The Metropolitan Museum of Art, Bequest of Samuel A. Lewisohn, 1951.)

Right: Attic Vase. *C.* 530–520 B.C. Red-figured Amphora. Attributed to the Andokides Painter. (The Metropolitan Museum of Art, Purchase, 1963. Joseph Pulitzer Bequest.)

Above: While all forms are bound into the plane there is a tendency inherent in them to push and grow into volumes which want to expand into depth.
Giotto: "Annunciation." Detail. (Fresco in the Scrovengi Chapel, Padua. 1304–1305.)

149

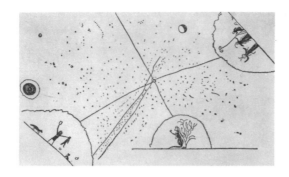

Left: Infinite space is compressed into this map of sun, moon, and the Pleiades and, in the center, the polestar from which the four directions originate. The Milky Way runs toward the World of Dawn. Opposite are the Evening and his Family. Between the two, darkness emerges from a tree.
Chukchi drawing. Eastern Siberia. A representation of the universe. (Musée de l'Homme, Paris.)

Center left: Suddenly, the brown color which denotes a total area of autumn becomes, also, a single leaf. The white outline lifts the brown from the "background" into the "foreground," from the general into the specific.
Paul Klee: "Last Leaves." Pastel on cotton. 1934. (Galerie Beyeler, Basle.)

Below: Things which, in "reality," are far apart in space and time—such as blossom and fruit, the crescent moon and the full moon—are drawn into one ideogram representing the process of growth.
Bark painting from Yirrkalla. Arnheim Land, Australia. (Australian Institute of Anatomy, Canberra.)

Right: The "empty" space between the elements of the branching-out structure is part of the whole. Space is conceived of and used as a medium; it is

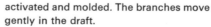

activated and molded. The branches move gently in the draft.
Alexander Calder: "Big Mobile in the International Arrival Building of J.F.K. Airport, New York." 1957.

Opposite: Space is treated as something at once permeable and permeating; it plays with solid forms, animates and is animated. An array of energies, including light and motion, is called together to create a total environment.
Nicolas Schoeffer: "Lux 10." Brass and copper, with lumino-dynamic projections; motorized. 1959. (Galerie Denise René, Paris.)

If the journey of the mind in meditation could be recorded, the tracing might look like this intricate and dense web of linear elements. Space and time become synonymous in this evocation of the shimmering night sky.

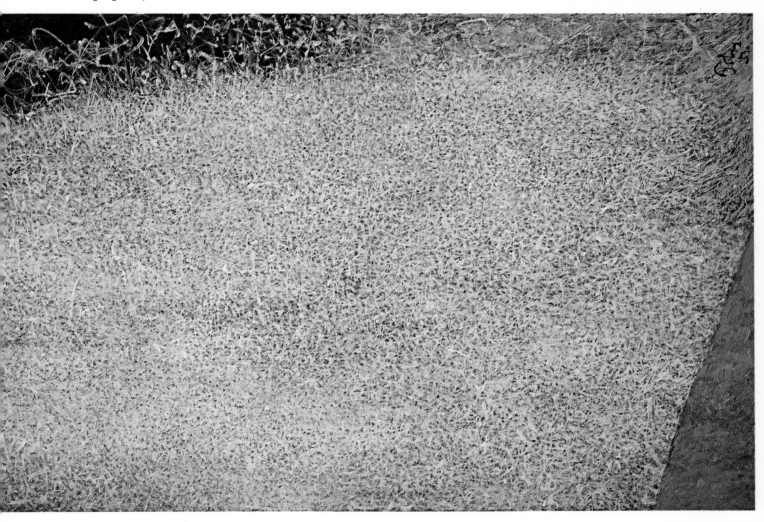

Mark Tobey: "Edge of August." Casein on composition board. 1953. (Collection, The Museum of Modern Art, New York. Purchase.)

ACKNOWLEDGMENTS

Most of the picture material in this book first appeared in a series of exhibitions assembled by the author for the Geigy Chemical Corp., Ardsley, New York.

Neither those exhibitions, nor this publication, would have been possible without the conviction, steadfast commitment, and enthusiasm of the company's president, Charles A. Suter.

The author had valuable suggestions and encouragement from Fred Troller and from Markus Loew, who nursed each exhibit through from its condition as a batch of illustrations to the actual display on the wall.

Special thanks are due to The Viking Press's Bryan Holme for his unending care and assistance in maintaining the concept of the book throughout the inevitable changes, and to Elizabeth Capelle for collecting reproductions and for stimulating comment.

I owe a great debt to Mr. Emil Buhrer of C. J. Bucher Ltd., Lucerne, for the understanding and daring he put into the layout; he proved to be the ideal interpreter of my intentions. Thanks are also due Mrs. Francine Tobler who made available picture material and hunted down, literally, many a rabbit for me.

It is my pleasure to acknowledge the assistance of André Ratti in his capacity as my agent as well as my friend. I have received editorial help from friends, amongst whom must be particularly acknowledged Suzanne Zelnick Gould and Mariette von Meyenburg.